*Secrets of Successful
Brides*

SECRETS OF SUCCESSFUL

BRIDES

*Brides Share Wedding Wisdom
on How They Did It*

SUZANNE KRESSE

St. Martin's Press \ New York

Design by Jaye Zimet

Library of Congress Cataloging-in-Publication Data

Kresse, Suzanne.
  Secrets of successful brides / Suzanne Kresse.
    p.   cm.
  Includes bibliographical references.
  ISBN 0-312-10538-X
  1. Weddings—Planning.   2. Wedding etiquette.   I. Title.
HQ745.K7   1994
395'.22—dc20   93-37877
                                                     CIP

First edition: February 1994
10   9   8   7   6   5   4   3   2   1

To my mother,
my guardian angel

Acknowledgments

Grateful appreciation is sent to the thousands of brides and their families across America who shared their wedding planning experiences to give new brides the advantage of their learned wisdom.

Thank you to my many friends and professional associates in the National Bridal Industry for their helpful references, statistics, and product information.

Special notes of gratitude go to my assistant, Debbie Otto, for her contributive opinions and fabulous technical skills, and to my editor, Jennifer Weis, for her expert attention to detail.

Contents

Introduction

Each year, as I conduct my wedding seminars across America, I meet over 100,000 brides. Afraid and confused, they seek perfection. They plan their weddings in the same traditional ways because they are not aware of all the options that are available to them. They search for references, asking "How did other brides do it?"

Now, for the first time ever, here is a resource of invaluable advice about the subjects that you, the bride of the '90s, are most concerned about. Through the real-life experiences recounted in this book, you will discover what actually happened when other brides fulfilled their dream wedding plans. Moreover, you will discover that their problems are very similar to yours, and you are not alone in your quest for perfection.

Here is the source you can constantly refer to—not only for what to do, but for how to do it. This ready reference will save you valuable time and money. Like no other planner, its learned wisdom will help you to avoid trouble and prevent tragedy. Feel free to write in the margins of this book and make your own special notes. This is the one book of wedding know-how that you should not be without.

CHAPTER 1

Some Engaging Stories

ENGAGEMENT FACTS TO KNOW

1. Announce the Engagement to Parents First.
2. Tell All Children Involved.
3. Notify Friends and Co-workers Last.
4. Select the Wedding Date.
5. Decide Whether to Have an Engagement Party.
6. Send Wedding Announcement to Local Newspapers.
7. Send Thank-you Notes for Any Engagement Gifts.
8. Send Special Note of Thanks and/or Gift to Anyone Who Hosts an Engagement Party for You.

When a woman says "yes," she officially begins her ascent to the altar. This chapter provides basic ring-buying advice and recounts the unique and funny ways that people successfully said "I do." Experiences connected with having an engagement party and placing engagement notices in the newspapers are included.

Sara, of Seattle, relives her thrilling engagement experience.

I know brides who are reading my story understand the thrill I felt when my fiancé proposed. What I want to tell them is that I felt that thrill all over again at our engagement party. The engagement party is really an optional event in the schedule of prewedding parties, but I am the oldest child and the first grandchild and my family wanted to savor every part of this first-time event in our family. My parents planned a backyard barbecue, but we kept the engagement a secret. We invited only our immediate families. After everyone arrived, my dad and mom came out of the house each holding a glass of champagne. My brothers followed with trays of the same and handed a glass to all. Then the big moment came. My dad and mom announced how thrilled they were to toast my fiancé and me in honor of our engagement. Oohs and ahs followed with clapping and lots of hugs (and tears). My fiancé returned the toast by saying that he was proud to join two wonderful families together. During the party we also called my grandmother who lives in Illinois so that she would feel included. This was one of the most memorable parts of my entire wedding planning.

A wedding announcement in the newspaper is considered a document of family history as well as a public notice of the status change. What brides don't know is that many papers publish this announcement FREE.

Claire, of Boston, shares some important newspaper facts.

From my own experience, I suggest that brides send in the wedding details and their picture at least two weeks before the wedding date. Don't be surprised if the announcement doesn't appear right away. I discovered that papers usually print announcements together, either in a special section or in a weekend edition of the paper. Most important, don't assume that the newspaper will mail you a complimentary copy when your announcement appears. It's up to you to watch for it and purchase as many copies as you need.

Barbara, of Albuquerque, has a clever engagement announcement idea.

I want to share an engagement idea that all of our family and friends thought was very clever. We took several posed pictures of ourselves smiling while in each other's arms. We took the best one to a copy center and had color copies printed on the backs of postcards. On the front side we announced our "big day." We sent this to all of our long-distance friends and relatives so that everyone could "meet" my fiancé and have advance notice to plan vacation time for attending our wedding.

Kelly, of Cincinnati, asks should she or shouldn't she return the engagement ring?

If an engagement is simply a public announcement that two people plan to marry, then I have really been engaged for five years. An engagement ring is not essential to make it official, but it helps. So when my fiancé bought me a ruby ring last Christmas and told me that it was my engagement ring, I was thrilled. That was six months ago. Today we are apart. All plans to marry have been called off. Now my fiancé wants the ring back! I refused. If he had given it to me when he originally asked me to get married, I could understand that it should be returned. But this was a dual-purpose gift—Christmas and as a sign of his "lasting love." I considered this ring to be a gift, and I do not feel that I should give it back.

There are many opinions about "who keeps the ring." Some say that if the woman breaks the engagement, she should return the ring; however, if the man breaks it, she is entitled to keep it as consolation. It is in better taste for the bride to return it. It is also proper to return all engagement and wedding gifts that have been received. In the event of a fiancé's death, an heirloom engagement ring should be returned to his family or mother, unless they insist that you keep it.

BRIDAL BARGAIN

Do you know a close friend or relative who is also engaged? See if she would like to have a double wedding. It's twice as much fun and half the cost.

Rochelle, of Brooklyn, explains why a band of gold is a wedding tradition every bride should consider.

My fiancé and I are graduating from college this June. After he proposed, we discussed wedding rings and decided to exchange matching bands. The jeweler told us that this custom began during World War II and really became popular again during the Persian Gulf War. He said that matching rings means "commitment whether together or separated." What really surprised me is that wedding bands are not always just plain gold but sculptured, clustered, and they can even include small diamonds or gemstones. I had always dreamed of receiving a diamond engagement ring, so I was delighted to know that I would wear a diamond-embellished wedding band. And as a symbol of our engagement, my fiancé surprised me with a precious diamond pendant on a gold chain. I feel like I have the best of both worlds.

There are so many styles of wedding bands to choose from, it's no wonder that you rarely run into another person wearing one identical to yours.

Mary, of Des Plaines, Illinois, tells about the special significance of engraved rings.

Some couples have their initials and wedding date engraved inside, but for my fiancé and me it was a way of exchanging a special secret message we alone understood. Our jeweler told us of other people's messages such as, "I will always love you. Forever, your Teddy Bear," and "I only have Ice for you." I feel that this has made our love very special.

Laura, of Washington, D.C., explains how every bride can have her "dazzling" diamond.

I always wanted a "rock" to wear on the third finger of my left hand. Unfortunately my husband was just finishing law school. He wanted to give me a beautiful ring, but he didn't have the money. According to budget guidelines, the groom should spend no more than 6 percent of his annual income for the engagement ring. By those standards, my "rock" suddenly turned into a "pebble," until we found out about the "royal cut" stones that are now available throughout America. Because the weight of the stone is

> **BRIDE BEWARE**
>
> *Shop only at reputable jewelers. When purchasing your diamond engagement ring, get a written guarantee indicating the value of the stone. This is called an appraisal. Then go to another reputable jeweler and get another written appraisal. If the second appraisal is more than 10 percent less than the price you paid, return your ring for a full refund.*

put at the top of the ring, the stone appears 50 percent bigger than a stone of the same weight in a traditional cut. My fiancé is happy because the ring is paid for, and I am thrilled because I am wearing a real dazzler. We made sure to get a written appraisal of the stone's value. One important thing we also learned is that the jewelry store will finance the ring but charges 18 to 24 percent, which is similar to what some major charge cards charge, while banks and credit unions charge approximately 12 percent because they use the ring as collateral for a secured loan.

This story not only has a happy ending, it makes great $ense.

Susan, of Dallas, relates the unusual way in which she was asked the "M" word.

I know that people have become engaged in many unique ways, but I think my "high-tech" film proposal is the most novel way I have ever heard of to ask the "M" word. My boyfriend had picked up a film at the video store. I thought we were going to watch the latest Bruce Willis flick. Instead, the film started and then the screen went blank. Suddenly there was my fiancé's face superimposed on Danny Aiello's body in the proposal scene of the movie *Moonstruck*. How could I refuse!

Marriage proposals can be verbal, written, or carried to extremes. Some other highly original proposals include:

Steve and Julie were parked in his old jalopy on a romantic starlit night. Steve turned on the car radio, which usually took a few minutes to warm up. He took Julie's hand, looked deeply into her eyes, and then suddenly something flew into his eye. He jumped, opened his eye wider, and kept repeating, "What's in my eye, what's in my eye?" As they grappled to find the foreign matter, the radio went on. The song was "The Look of Love Is in Your Eye." They both burst into laughter. Then Steve looked into Julie's eyes and said, "Let's get married."

Don asked Marie, "How would you like my mother to be your mother-in-law?"

WEDDING LORE

In olde England, a betrothal party called a "flouncing" was held so that a newly engaged couple could meet friends of both families. The "flouncing" established a formal contract and marked an abrupt status change. From that time on, the couple could not be seen with or talking to other suitors. If either changed his or her mind about the marriage, the other could claim half of his or her property.

THE WORLD'S LONGEST ENGAGEMENT

The longest engagement on record was between Octavio Guillen and Adriana Martinez. After 67 years, they finally took the plunge in June 1969 in Mexico City. Both were 82 years old on their wedding day.

—Guinness Book of World Records

James put his proposal in lights on the scoreboard at a local hockey game.

Mark took Kathy for an airplane ride in a rented plane so she could read his words of love on a rooftop.

Gary took out a full-page ad in their community newspaper.

Sam placed a special message in Sandi's fortune cookie.

John hired a message service to send "Cupid" to deliver his proposal of love.

Kevin rented a suit of armor and a horse, and rode to his lovely damsel's house to ask for her hand.

Jerry was so "ape" over Connie he rented a 25-foot inflatable gorilla, set it up on his front lawn, and plastered a "Will you marry me?" sign across its chest.

Gary hired an airplane pilot to fly his banner of love across the sky in front of Melanie's office window.

Richard arranged with Debbie's beauty salon operator to give her a luxurious manicure and to finish by giving her a small box. There was a special note from him inside.

Ralph asked Cheryl to help him baby-sit for his nephews. When she arrived at their home, 25 people all holding "Will you marry me?" signs stood in the living room. Ralph was in the center. His sign asked "Please?" Cheryl's resounding answer was "Yes."

Jim gave Barbara a jar of jewelry cleaner in which the diamond ring was found.

Harry gave Nicole a new name plate for her desk with her "to-be" married name on it.

Fred placed a portable lit up sign with his message of love on Bonnie's front lawn.

David placed Sue's diamond ring in a box of chocolate letters that read "Will you marry me?"

Worst Wedding Worries

1. *Money, and not enough of it, is the biggest wedding worry.*
2. *Concern about whether the couple is making the right decision.*
3. *Fear that the excitement of their love will not last.*
4. *Anxiety over whether they are ready to give up the single life.*
5. *Concern about getting along with in-laws.*
6. *Worry about following proper wedding protocol.*
7. *Worry about a breakdown in communication.*
8. *Fear that the marriage will not last.*
9. *Anxiety about birth control.*
10. *Confusion about career obligations and whether they will interfere with the marriage.*

Phil arranged to have the waiter bring out a dozen roses followed by a cassette player that played "their song" as he asked Marni to be his bride.

Joe made Jenny go on a scavenger hunt and follow the "clues" that led to finding her engagement ring.

As far back as the 15th century, when a woman was "betrothed" to a man, a ring was given as an official symbol of their intent to marry. Although the wording may have changed, the symbolic engagement ring has remained. Like moonlight and love songs, the romance of getting engaged will never go out of style.

CHAPTER 2

Parents and Money

Bride's Parents

1. Invite Groom's Parents to Meet and Begin Wedding Planning.
2. Prepare a Guest List.
3. Host an Engagement Party.
4. Offer to Assist in Planning and Paying for as Many Items as You Can Afford.
5. Pay for Your Own Wedding Attire.
6. Attend the Wedding Rehearsal.
7. Attend the Rehearsal Dinner.
8. Participate in the Ceremony.
9. Serve as "Official" Hosts and Hostesses at the Reception Party. Help in Any Manner Necessary.
10. Give the Couple a Special Wedding Gift That Is as Generous or as Simple as Affordable.
11. Take Care of Wedding Gifts and Any Other "After-the-Wedding" Jobs While the Bridal Couple Is Honeymooning.

OPTION:

12. Host a "Gift-Opening" Party the Day After the Wedding.

(CONTINUED)

Groom's Parents

1. Call the Bride's Parents to Express Happiness About Engagement.
2. Prepare a Guest List.
3. Attend the Engagement Party if Possible and Provide a Special Gift.
4. Offer to Assist in Planning and Paying for as Many Items as You Can Afford.
5. Pay for Your Own Wedding Attire.
6. Attend the Wedding Rehearsal.
7. Attend the Rehearsal Dinner.
8. Participate in the Ceremony.
9. Serve as "Official" Hosts and Hostesses at the Reception Party. Help in Any Manner Necessary.
10. Give the Couple a Special Wedding Gift That Is as Generous or as Simple as Affordable.
11. Take Care of Any Other "After-the-Wedding" Jobs Necessary While the Bridal Couple Is Honeymooning.

This chapter deals with the two hardest obstacles to overcome when planning a wedding. It is divided into three sections because of the real-life situations that exist today. First, it provides guidelines about the duties of natural parents. It also features unique suggestions for when parents are deceased. Second, it offers new ways to handle "divorced parent" situations. Finally, it focuses on wedding expenses and how couples overcome the "high costs" of getting married in the '90s.

Section 1

As the official hosts and hostesses of the wedding party, it is up to the parents of the bridal couple to introduce people, circulate among the guests, talk to members of the "other side of the family," and, in general, make everyone feel at home.

For Sharon, of St. Louis, her wedding was also a special day for her parents. To pay tribute to them for all they had done for her, she honored them in a very special way.

My parents celebrated their thirtieth wedding anniversary on the day of my wedding. To give them something special, we proposed a special toast to them after the best man's toast, and everyone rose and clapped. After our first dance, we had the band leader announce their favorite song and allowed them to dance alone. After they had danced a short while, my in-laws joined in and were followed by the rest of the bridal party. For me, this was a very touching memory that inspired me to strive for commitment in my marriage.

This is a great idea for other brides who may be wondering what to do for this or a similar situation.

Helen, of Philadelphia, suggests a unique yet inexpensive thank-you for parents.

According to etiquette books, we owed it to our parents to send them a gift of thanks after the wedding. We did not have a lot of money left once everything was paid for so we decided to propose a special toast of thanks to both of our parents at our reception dinner. We followed that by sending each of them a special telegram a few days later.

Just a special card of thanks or simply a note written from the heart sent to them a few days after the celebration would also show how much you appreciate them.

Lynn, of Peoria, Illinois, incorporated her mother's special talent into her wedding celebration.

My mother has a beautiful voice and has been a soloist at other weddings. I featured her at our ceremony by having her sing a song. It was a very touching and wonderful way to add her special talent to my special day.

Sylvia, the mother of a bride in Atlanta, wants other mothers to profit from her big mistake.

My best advice to mothers about wedding planning is to "*Think* before you speak." So many details puts everyone under pressure and words can *hurt*. I imposed my own ideas on my daughter's wedding to the point of even trying to get her to pick the china pattern I thought was the best looking. You don't realize, or expect, all of the chaos and emotional turmoil that can build. It's the little things—who sits where, who's invited to the shower—that get blown out of proportion. It was my daughter who finally straightened everything, including me, out. "Mom," she said, "you know this is my special day and I want to be happy. I know you love me and want me to be happy too. Let's work together, *but* I must make the final decision." She was absolutely right!

Wedding planning can be a real team effort for you and your mother as long as you remember one simple rule—you've got to communicate.

Agnes, the mother of a bride from Houston, shares some insight about visiting wedding guests.

I'm sorry that we had friends and relatives stay with us during the days before the wedding. We had so much to do, making phone calls and putting the finishing touches on all the wedding details, I didn't have time to spend with or entertain my out-of-town relatives.

Using local relatives to keep out-of-towners occupied can be a tremendous help. It is also advisable that no additional relatives stay at the bride's home, simply because the solitude of just your immediate family will help to keep everyone's nerves calm, especially during those last 48 hours before the big day.

Marlene, of Tulsa, Oklahoma, suggests novel ideas to get in-laws more involved.

My mother was helping me every minute of every day in planning my wedding. My father's special job, besides licking stamps and making pickups, was to escort me down the aisle. My fiancé's parents, however, had provided their guest list and were just waiting for further orders. We decided to put my father-in-law in charge of the refreshments, what we would serve, bartenders, et cetera. We also had him add his special touch to our ceremony by doing a reading. My mother-in-law and my mother lit the unity candle at our ceremony, and I invited my mother-in-law to go with us to several bridal shows. It was a lot of fun, and a great way for all of us to get to know each other better.

Rebecca, of Long Island, used ethnic traditions to honor her new in-laws.

My in-laws are Jewish. My father-in-law is a very successful man who values his ethnic origin highly. We put him in charge of the arrangements for the special customs and traditions they cherish. One custom, in particular, gave my mother-in-law a special place at our wedding. It is called the *Die Mezinke Ausgegeben*, which means that when the last child in a family marries, the Jewish mother is honored by being seated in the center of a circle while the guests dance around her. Guests may also present her with flowers during this dance.

Lisa, of Memphis, related her "in-law" trouble. It may help you to avoid a wedding day disaster.

Both my parents and my fiancé's parents contributed financially to our wedding. But my mother-in-law started criticizing everything from the moment we announced our engagement. Finally, my fiancé told her to "butt out." On the day of our

---

WEDDING LORE

In 18th-century England, mothers-in-law believed that if they broke a loaf of bread over their daughter-in-law's head as she entered the newlywed's home, happiness for the married couple was assured.

wedding, my fiancé's father arrived at the church alone. Red-faced, he explained that his wife was "sick" and could not attend. My fiancé was so upset that he immediately called her and got into a shouting match over the phone. It appeared that since she was told to butt out, she assumed that this included not coming to the wedding. This put a terrible gloom on our whole wedding day, and my husband and I ended up in a huge argument about her in front of everyone. Since the wedding, almost one year ago, I have developed a polite tolerance for her, as she has since sunk her fangs into my husband's brother and his new fiancée.

When parents give financial support, they sometimes feel that they have decision powers based on their contributions. While it is definitely your wedding, and you should plan it the way you want it, you should not make unilateral rulings without considering the ideas and preferences of your families, who are, after all, also an integral part of your wedding. It would have been wise for Lisa to sit down with her future mother-in-law to talk things out and set up ground rules that everyone could agree to. This kind of team effort would have given the mother-in-law guidelines and may have eliminated the hurt that built up and produced this wedding day disaster.

Katie, of Long Beach, California, tells how her domineering mother caused her wedding day anguish.

For over two years, I lived across the country from my parents and my hometown in New York. I fell in love and just wanted to get married. My mother insisted that I have a big showy wedding. I cringed when she sent me a huge check in the mail and persisted in her eagerness to plan a gala event. It reached the point where I had to get even. When she arrived, she saw, to her horror, that I had bought an obviously second-hand tattered taffeta gown, rented a lower-level bowling alley for the reception, and marched up the aisle with my dog as my maid of honor, complete with a "doggy" dress. All of the fabulous details were beautifully photographed as a keepsake memento of her insensitive disregard for my feelings or desires. I have not spoken with her since that day—a little over one year ago.

Planning a purposely staged "wedding of spite" could not have been a very happy day for this bride either. This story should have had a happy ending. The mother's intentions were honorable. She wanted the best for her daughter. If the best, in her daughter's mind, was a simple affair, that is what the mother should have paid for. She should have been happy keeping her daughter's happiness foremost in her mind. Brides and parents—communicate! Communicate! Communicate!

Dolores, the mother of a bride from Minneapolis, has wonderful advice for those last days before the wedding.

Lay low. Brides are usually uptight before the wedding day. They're ready to hit the ceiling every time you even look at them. If you mothers keep a calm, low profile at home, they'll settle down. It really works! After the wedding, my daughter thanked me for "keeping her from going crazy."

Another way to reduce stress is to use a good wedding planning book and follow its schedule. If you're organized, you will relax. When little fumbles happen, you'll be able to take them in stride.

Mary Anne, of Phoenix, offers a unique idea for special elderly relatives.

My grandmother was in the hospital and my great-aunt was in a nursing home. Neither of them could attend the wedding. To make sure they knew we were thinking of them, we decorated a basket with ribbons in our wedding colors and filled it with wedding cake and little keepsakes. My parents delivered it to each of them the day after our wedding. When we returned from our honeymoon we visited them and took along the video and honeymoon photos so that they could see all of the excitement and happiness of the day.

Bill, of Chicago, expressed the father's general point of view.

Nobody's paying much attention to me today. But I can assure you that I am getting my special share of attention. The banks and several businesses are watching me very closely.

Do get your father involved. Everyone thinks that Dad doesn't want to be bothered, but in truth, he is one person who knows both you and your fiancé well. Since he's probably not intimately involved in the preparations, he could be the best referee around.

Karl, of Fort Wayne, Indiana, had these moving words of wisdom to say.

We all know real men don't cry. But when my daughter walked down the aisle last month, my eyes flooded their banks and I spent the rest of the ceremony reaching into my wife's box of Kleenex. I cried because, seeing my daughter there, in a beautiful gown with a long train and roses in her hands and a beautiful glow on her face, filled me with a joy that was too big, too good, to keep inside. I cried because she looked so exquisitely happy with her hand being held close by the man she loves and this was the most special moment in her life so far. I cried, most of all, because that's my little girl who was standing there, and she's all grown up now and she's beautiful and bright and ready to start her own life. I'm proud that we did a heck of a job getting her ready for that. Did all of this crying make me less than a man? Hey, pal, if you think so, let's you and I step outside.

Sally, of Madison, Wisconsin, thought innovatively about how to include her disabled father, and came up with this solution:

My dad is confined to a wheelchair. I love him very much and wanted him to be a part of my wedding. We know that our church has an extremely long aisle, so we worried about his ability to wheel himself all that way. At the dress rehearsal, we practiced with our priest's assistance. We resolved the situation by having the head usher wheel my dad halfway down the aisle after the bridesmaids had proceeded. I then began my processional alone and met him, at which point, we walked together to the altar where he transferred my hand from his to my fiancé's, and I gave him a kiss. During this time, the head usher had positioned himself at the altar entrance ready to wheel Dad back to his seat. It was just beautiful.

As a suggestion for the reception family dance, which may also be a concern, simply dance the first dance with your new husband and then invite everyone else to join you on the dance floor. There is no mandatory roster listing whom family members must dance with.

Penny, of Savannah, honored her deceased grandfather at her wedding.

My grandfather had passed away three months before my wedding. In his honor, we placed a bouquet of his favorite flowers, tulips, on the altar. We then explained their presence in our wedding program.

While it is a gesture of honor to remember special deceased loved ones at the wedding, it can also renew mourning for others in the family, causing a renewal of sadness that may have just started to be recovered from. Be considerate of deceased loved ones, but be more concerned about the living relatives who are present at this joyous occasion to celebrate your happiness. If necessary, ask the widows or widowers about memorial ideas first.

Tammi, of Springfield, Ohio, included a family heirloom in her traditional wedding.

On my wedding day, I wore my grandmother's locket, which my mother had inherited after her death. It was a very special "something old" to include in my wedding attire.

Section 2

This section focuses on divorced parents and the special problems that can develop when a wedding is being planned with important people who are at odds with each other. Whether parents are divorced or not, there is one rule that everyone should follow: This is the bride and groom's day. All parents should be willing to cooperate to make that day enjoyable.

Ways to keep things running smoothly when divorced parents are involved:
1. Pay for the wedding yourselves.
2. Choose a neutral site that will not awaken painful memories.
3. Invite as many people as possible. (It's easy to get lost in crowds.)

4. Serve a buffet at the reception, thereby eliminating any need for a formal seating plan.

Best Advice:

5. Keep a comfortable distance between the parents.

Julie, of Detroit, discovered a simple situation for a complex parent problem.

My parents put me in the center of a tug-of-war about planning my wedding. From the size of the wedding to the seating plan, they continued to be at odds. Finally I realized that they weren't really arguing about the plans as much as seeing who was going to win. That's when I took the reins and made the rest of the decisions by myself.

It is best to clear the air with parents and then give them the space they need. Usually they will cooperate for their children's sake.

Elaine, of Orlando, shares her secret for keeping out of in-law trouble.

My fiancé's parents are divorced. I simply let him handle them, by himself, throughout the planning process. I stayed out of it, so we didn't fight and everything worked out well.

Cindi, of Cleveland, tells how a little understanding can go a long way.

My father, who is divorced from my mother, is the one who could not put his differences aside. He refused to attend the wedding because my mother was bringing another man. I told him that I understood his feelings, and while I respected his decision, I really hoped he would change his mind.

Don't let divorced parents use your wedding as a power struggle.

Luann, of Little Rock, used professional helpers for her divorced parents.

Our photographer, an experienced wedding professional, really helped us handle the formal family pictures. We did take a picture with my divorced parents together, but they stood one on each side of my husband and myself. It was short and sweet and no one was made to feel uncomfortable about it. The photographer also took photos of my husband and me with each parent separately. These are the keepsake photos we gave to them so that no painful memories would be awakened.

Avoid awkward situations at your wedding by explaining your parents' marital status to all wedding professionals, including the caterer, clergy, and especially the photographer.

Janine, of Billings, Montana, found that counseling helped greatly for her mother.

My mother, divorced and alone, really put a guilt trip on me about leaving her to get married. We had several talks together but ended up going to a counselor to help her with her anxieties. I had allowed her to become so dependent on me that my marriage caused a real emotional loss.

When a woman marries, she transfers loyalty from her family to her new husband. This doesn't mean that she abandons her parents, it's just that her loyalties must shift. Caring parents will help their daughter ease into that transition. Professional counseling can be very helpful at times in making that adjustment.

Shirley, of Hamilton, Mississippi, explains an unusual in-law arrangement.

My fiancé's parents had been divorced and remarried for some time. He lived with his grandparents for over twelve years, so he decided to have his grandfather as his best man, and his grandmother took his mother's place during our ceremony and reception. His parents were also invited, and they were seated separately a few rows behind his grandmother. His grandparents were thrilled to be honored, and his parents didn't mind taking a backseat.

When parents and bridal couples cooperate, the wedding always has a happy ending!

Kathy, of Birmingham, Alabama, asks, "Flowers for one or flowers for all?"

Because of the number of relatives that accumulated with sequential marriages in our families, it became too costly for us to provide corsages for several "mothers" and numerous "grand-mothers." Our florist offered two viable options. Either purchase flowers only for the members of the original families, or purchase more elaborate flowers for the original family and simple one-flower corsages for members of the sequential families.

Judith, the stepmother of a bride from San Francisco, explains that composure and dignity saved her stepdaughter's wedding day.

My husband's daughter from his first marriage was recently wed at her mother's home in an immediate-family-only affair. I had never met this woman, but she had caused many problems in the first few years of our marriage. I was very nervous, but I went to the wedding, for my husband's sake. I also would never have insulted my stepdaughter, who lived with us for several years during her rebellious teens. I said "hello" when we were introduced and remained as far away from her as possible throughout the event. It was not easy.

Your behavior is to be commended. It is an insult to purposely not go to someone's home in a situation like this. If, on the other hand, you would have felt it was impossible for you to remain polite, then the proper thing would have been to allow your husband to attend alone.

THREE SIMPLE WAYS TO SAVE ON WEDDING EXPENSES

1. *Trim your guest list (five to ten names can save a lot).*
2. *Consider having fewer attendants in your bridal party.*
3. *Make your honeymoon plans when special air fare programs are advertised.*

Section 3

This section discusses wedding expenses. The wedding of the '90s is a shared expense. No longer does the bride's family pay for the entire affair. Rather, the bridal couple themselves pay for most of the costs, and parents, on each side, help to whatever extent they can. This section also illustrates how money problems have been solved and gives examples of how weddings were budgeted.

Dan, the father of a bride from Nashville, realized that it takes money—and lots of it—to make a "dream wedding" a reality.

I remarked that I knew I had to give the bride away, but I didn't know that she had to be gift-wrapped!

A wedding budget is a necessity. While there are no set money rules, any agreed-upon arrangements between the immediate families are acceptable.

Alexandra, of Chattanooga, Tennessee, warns others to be wary of promises that may or may not materialize.

When we became engaged, we planned an intimate supper party with our parents to talk about the wedding. My mom and dad agreed to give us a certain amount toward the expenses. My fiancé's mother promised to pay for the rehearsal dinner. She was also going to contribute toward the overall expenses. The company she worked for was giving her a trip, and she offered it to us for our honeymoon. We were thrilled. As the wedding drew nearer, our budget was being stretched, but we felt we would be able to handle it. Then the boom fell. The company my future mother-in-law worked for folded and her promised trip went out the window. She did not have the money to give us for the honeymoon, so she had to face us and tell us what had happened and that she was very sorry. I was angry. We had to get an extra loan in order to go to Jamaica. Secretly, I really never forgave my mother-in-law for that disappointment.

While it is wrong to mislead or disappoint loved ones who are counting on your promises, companies are folding left and right. Your mother-in-law was sincere in her intention to give you her trip. She should not be blamed for something beyond her control. Perhaps choosing a less expensive, exotic honeymoon location might have lessened the added expense you had to incur.

Jack, the father of a bride from Rochester, Minnesota, reflects on his expensive wedding walk.

I am the divorced father of the bride. I have supported my daughter throughout her life. I escorted her down the aisle, but that privilege cost me $5,000.

If you have the money, consider it a good investment, and your special wedding role—one of life's greatest privileges. If you don't have the money, be honest about it, and offer whatever help you can.

Toby, of Laguna Beach, California, shares her thoughts about "joint" financial responsibilities.

My fiancé's parents offered to pay for part of our wedding. I was truly grateful, but felt a bit embarrassed. To make things easier, my fiancé and I suggested that they choose the orchestra, the photographer, or the refreshments—whichever one they wished, to help us with. I felt this eliminated any awkwardness about what the amount of their contribution should be. As it turned out, they paid for both the orchestra and the refreshments—plus the rehearsal dinner.

Wonderful contributions such as these always lead to a happy and successful wedding. Today, parents are not responsible for your wedding costs, and the groom's parents are not obligated to pay for anything.

Rhonda, of Boca Raton, describes the wedding outline she created.

I developed my own wedding outline as the written framework for my wedding celebration. It included:

1. The kind of wedding we wanted.
2. The kind of ceremony we wanted.
3. The number of people in our bridal party.
4. The best date and time for the wedding.
5. The reception sites we liked best (top 3).
6. The kind of reception party I wanted.
7. The type of meal and refreshments we wanted to serve.
8. The entertainment we wanted to include.

BRIDE BEWARE

Allow an additional 25 percent more money for the "extras" you haven't even thought of. This includes tips, wedding favors, hairdresser costs, and your presents to each other.

9. The estimated amount we could afford to spend.

It is also a good idea to keep all receipts and contracts organized by filing them in large envelopes according to categories.

Over 10 percent of brides nationwide say that their wedding creates a financial burden in their lives.

Nancy, of Needham, Massachusetts, tells how she avoided financial trouble.

I would like to suggest one way brides can save for their wedding. It worked wonderfully for us. My fiancé and I had our company credit unions set aside $60 from each of our paychecks. We had a $3,000 nest egg in one year without lifting a finger.

Banks can also transfer funds from your checking to your savings account in the same manner.

Kathryn, of Stamford, Connecticut, recommends building a nest egg as well.

My fiancé and I opened a special joint wedding saving account into which we deposited money monthly to pay for our wedding costs. We began making our wedding arrangements one year prior to the event. This nest egg of funds provided us with those necessary deposits that had to be given as we progressed with our plans.

This is a very helpful idea that every couple should consider. Today wedding businesses not only require a written purchase order or contract, they also demand a deposit to reserve that date for you alone.

Julie, of Little Rock, explains the credit card advantage.

Couples should check into the Arkansas Federal Credit Card, which offers an outstanding 8.5 percent interest rate. This credit card gave me and my fiancé purchasing power with a real advantage. The federal consumer protection laws guard all of our deposits and payments made with a credit card. (You must be planning your wedding in your home state and the purchase must be $50 or more.) But if for any reason you have a problem and try in

---

BRIDAL BARGAIN

Timing is everything—consider an off-season month (January through March) or an off night (Friday or Sunday) for savings of up to 50 percent.

WEDDING CONTRACT TIPS TO GUARANTEE YOU'LL GET WHAT YOU'VE PAID FOR:

1. *Sign a contract or letter of agreement with every vendor you use for your wedding.*
2. *List all details—including names, costs, dates, times—so you have records if anything goes wrong.*
3. *Signatures are vital. Both you and the vendors must sign the contract to make it legally binding.*
4. *Include a conditional rider. If the vendor can't perform, name the substitutes.*
5. *List all conditions for the return of your deposit—include a cancellation clause with date limitations.*

good faith to rectify it but cannot, you can contact your bank to request your full refund.

Another advantage of a credit card is that it allows you a grace period (usually 25 to 30 days) in which you can repay the bill without any interest.

The most important "to-do" for your wedding is to create a budget. First decide how much to spend and then how the expenses will be divided. Compromise on quantity, not quality, and keep the budget flexible enough so that unexpected expenses will not disrupt it.

CHAPTER 3

The Ceremony: Religious and Secular

CEREMONY FACTS TO KNOW

1. Ceremony Arrangements Should be Made on a Timely Basis So That They Coordinate With Reception Arrangements.
2. An Appointment With a Religious Office Is Necessary To:
   - View Facilities
   - Set the Date and Time of Wedding
   - Discuss Accessories and Fees
   - Discuss Rules About Photography and Videotaping
   - Discuss Musical Arrangements
   - Discuss Fees
   - Set the Rehearsal Date and Time
3. Prenuptial Counseling Is Usually Required for Any Ceremony Held in a Place of Worship.
4. Couples May Write Their Own Vows.
5. Favorite Songs, Special Instruments, and Soloists Must Be Discussed With the Accompanist.

This chapter offers facts to know about your ceremony arrange-
ments, annulments and alternatives, whether it is in a religious or
a secular setting. It talks about difficulties couples experienced in
fulfilling church requirements in order to be married there. It also
deals with divorced couples and the special problems they face.
Ceremony restrictions, including the costs and problems associated
with some religious officiants, are featured.

Jane, of Lake Geneva, Wisconsin, describes her grand ceremony entrance.

Our wedding took place outdoors on the front porch of a beautiful country club. The clubhouse has a huge circular drive and a large grassy area in the middle. Guests sat there and waited while a white Rolls-Royce drove in and around to the front door where I was greeted by my father, and helped out of the car and up the steps to my waiting groom and attendants. It was a different and wonderful experience.

Carol, of Indianapolis, suggests a "sporting" ceremony.

My husband and I are real sports nuts. We both love football so it was only natural that we wanted to do something unique and sporty for our wedding. We made arrangements through our college alumni office to hold our wedding on the 50-yard line of the school football field. We dressed in the locker rooms, had the school band provide the music, and all of our guests had front-row seats to our special ceremony. It was everything we hoped for—especially because our priest worked closely with us and even used some clever sports wording in his sermon.

Terry, of Denver, explains how she was "coached" not to tell about her premarital living arrangements.

My girlfriend warned me to give my parents' address as my home and not to tell the priest at our parish that I was living with my fiancé. My friend told me that her co-worker became disgusted because their pastor, upon knowing of their living arrangements, refused to allow them to be married in his church. They searched, told a fib, and made arrangements with another pastor so that they could be married at a religious ceremony in their faith.

> **BRIDAL BARGAIN**
>
> *Brides across America suggest that new brides contact others who will also marry at their church on their same date. If they can coordinate the color schemes of the church floral and candle decorations, they can save money by sharing the costs.*

Lynne, of Chicago, recalls the "word" rules she had to follow for her religious ceremony.

Both my husband and I work in the publishing industry. "Words" are very important to us. Accordingly, our vows were an extremely integral part of our remarriage ceremony. However, our priest required that traditional vows only be used. His philosophy was that the church was a sanctuary of God and unlike the words of a manuscript, the words of matrimonial bonding should not be altered or rewritten. He did, however, allow us to substitute phrases like "as long as we both shall love" instead of "live." We added some verses and even mentioned some close friends and family. We took our "script" to him for his review, which, with a few minor changes, he approved.

Tanja, of Columbus, asked, "Where's the priest?"

The ceremony was to start at 2:00 P.M. I was ready and waiting to walk down the aisle. The entire congregation had turned to watch. But, where was the priest? A search party was sent out, while the wedding party and guests sat, and the organist and soloist performed the same five songs over and over again. A replacement priest was located a half hour later. Supposedly the pastor, who had attended an out-of-town seminar, assumed that the assistant was planning to be there to officiate.

Father Callahan, also of Columbus, tells how his words of wedding wisdom have saved the day many times.

When planning the wedding with the bride and groom, I always ask their permission to make an announcement before the wedding. If they agree (and so far they all have), I walk out in front of the guests, the organist lowers the volume to almost nothing, then I say "My name is Pastor Paul, and I have two very important requests to make on behalf of the bride and groom: The first—please do not take any flash pictures during the ceremony; the second—if you have a small child who begins to cry, please do not wait, hoping the child will stop. Take the child out immediately so that others will be able to enjoy the ceremony." This has worked very well, underscoring an old adage: An ounce of prevention is worth a pound of cure.

WORLD'S LARGEST
WEDDING CEREMONY

The largest mass wedding ceremony was one of 6,516 couples officiated over by Sun Myung Moon (b. 1920) of the Holy Spirit Association for the Unification of World Christianity at a factory near Seoul, South Korea, on October 30, 1988.

—Guinness Book of World Records

Darlene, of El Paso, reminds brides that when you are married in the eyes of God, you are also married in the eyes of the law.

My husband gave our marriage license to our best man two days before our wedding. At the rehearsal dinner he quietly told my husband that he had misplaced it, but would keep looking for it until he found it. The next day, our wedding day, while guests were arriving at the church, he was still looking. As my tears ruined my makeup, the minister walked into the dressing room. I'll never forget his words. "I feel that I have come to know both you and Jim well. I also feel that the Lord would be pleased with your marriage. So, I will marry you in the eyes of God and your family today and in the eyes of the state on Tuesday. The ceremony was perfect until the last minute. I accidentally smacked my husband in the face with my bouquet as I turned to kiss him.

Your minister was very kind, as it is his legal obligation (the way it is in any state of the United States) to have a valid marriage license in his hand before any vows are exchanged.

Florence, of Waukegan, Illinois, has a great tip about tipping.

One concern we had about our wedding ceremony was how much to tip the minister. We did not want to insult somebody by giving him/her the wrong amount. Fortunately my aunt, who works in the city clerk's office, gave us the benefit of her experience. In a civil ceremony, the officiant's fee can range between $20 and $50. But some judges cannot accept any money, so it is a good idea to ask when you apply for the license. For a church ceremony, the best person to ask is the secretary. The tip is usually given by the best man in a sealed envelope following the ceremony.

Professionals who help to make your wedding day run smoother should be compensated. But sincere tipping is an individual expression of gratitude, so let your own good judgment dictate what you feel you want to give.

Jill, of Sacramento, says that lighting a unity candle was a meaningful part of the ceremony.

We felt that the unity candle ceremony was a wonderful tradition, and wanted to include it during our marriage ceremony,

WEDDING LORE

In ancient Eastern church ceremonies, the Holy Trinity played an important part. The wedding ring was placed first on the thumb "in the name of the Father"; next on the forefinger "and the Son"; then on the middle finger "and of the Holy Spirit"; and last, on the third finger "Amen."

as it symbolizes the spiritual uniting of two people. Both my husband and I each lit a single taper candle, then together, we lit a larger center candle using the two lighted flames.

Be sure to ask your clergyman if you can include this tradition in your ceremony. Some churches will even provide the candle holders.

Jessica, of Kenosha, Wisconsin, cautions brides to ask about any videotaping restrictions during the ceremony.

Photographing our ceremony, especially videotaping the exchange of our vows, was very important to my fiancé and me. Because of the structure of the altar area in my church, it was impossible for a video to be done without having the cameraman practically sit next to the priest. Our church would not allow this, and we ended up going to my husband's church where they could accommodate us, and did not mind doing so.

Wedding videos have become a necessity in our modern world of instant recall. Nothing can ever replay the moving memory of your exchange of vows, or your first kiss as husband and wife, like a video can. If this is important to you, it is your privilege to seek out different churches or other facilities whose officiants will cooperate with you.

Debbie, of Kansas City, Missouri, suggests you ask yourself how important your ceremony's musical selections are to you.

We planned a traditional religious service. We went through all the prenuptial counseling and really enjoyed the guidance and friendship that we developed with the priest, who is an associate at our church. Everything was fine until we talked about including contemporary songs that have special meaning to us in our service. We were told bluntly that this was a religious service being held in the house of God. Standards of respect and reverence had to be upheld, and the pastor reserved the right to approve or disapprove of any musical selection he felt was inappropriate.

If you cannot agree about the selection of musical works you want to include in your service, it is wise to consult with other officiants who may be more flexible.

Meredith, of Seattle, recalls:

I'm sorry that I did not talk to the singer about the prayers we wanted sung during our ceremony. She sang far too many psalms and prayers. I should have previewed her in the church and told her when and how often we wanted her to chime in. My husband almost stood up in the middle of the service and yelled "cut"!

It is up to you, the bridal couple, to ask for the name and phone number of the organist in order to meet with him/her to discuss the special songs and the use of other instruments or vocalists for your ceremony.

According to a recent national bridal magazine survey, 75 percent of all couples are marrying in a religious setting. When it comes to choosing a date, timing *is everything. With only 52 weeks in a given year, many couples who are interested in a special date find too often that religious facilities are all booked. Thus, they now bring the officiant to a unique secular setting such as a hotel, yacht, or private mansion. It is not the religious place at which your ceremony occurs that matters. Rather, it is the person who officially marries you in a religious ceremony that counts.*

Debbie, of Pittsburgh, illustrates this growing '90s wedding trend.

My fiancé and I met on New Year's Eve. We became engaged on the following New Year's Eve. We wanted to be married on that day also. We are practicing Catholics, but we were very disappointed to find that because New Year's Day is a holy day in our religion, our church would not marry anyone on the eve of a church holiday. Then my mother-in-law suggested that we hold our festive holiday wedding at a hotel, including the ceremony itself. We found a priest to officiate, and everything worked out beautifully. Not only did we love our elegant candlelight ceremony, we saved the travel time between the church and the reception hall. In addition, all of our out-of-town guests stayed at this hotel and enjoyed the hotel's facilities. At midnight, our guests received party hats, horns, streamers, and a huge shower

BRIDE BEWARE

Ask only an accomplished singer or musician to take part in your service. Only one thing is worse than no music at all, and that's bad music.

WORLD'S OLDEST BRIDE AND GROOM

The oldest recorded bridegroom is Harry Stevens, age 103, who married Thelma Lucas, age 84, at the Caravilla Retirement Home in Wisconsin on December 3, 1984.

—Guinness Book of World Records

of balloons that ended the old year and began our new married life—exactly the way we dreamed it would happen.

Tiffany, of Northbrook, Illinois, relates important information about another growing phenomenon.

When my fiancé, who had attended Catholic school for 12 years, announced that he intended to marry me, a Jewish girl, his parents told him to leave home. They refused to attend our wedding, which was held at my home. It really hurt us a lot, but we loved each other. We were united in a "neutral" religious service. The ceremony itself was written by us in conjunction with a wonderful clergymember who became our guide and ally. We chose to reflect and emphasize our cooperative view of our interfaith marriage. Instead of using a standard wedding text, we edited references that we felt might be offensive to members of the other religion and concentrated instead on the similarities between the two. It is almost a year now since our wedding day. Only recently did my husband and his parents begin to make tentative gestures of reconciliation. It has been a difficult situation to overcome.

Today, about 50 percent of all Catholics and at least 33 percent of Jews marry outside of their religions. Many Protestants marry outside of their religion as well as their denominations. Surveys compiled from major religious sect records show that 80 percent of Americans today approve of interfaith marriages. In essence, every marriage is mixed because faith means something different to every person.

Joyce, of Cleveland, narrates her tale of the long "red tape."

I was married in a Catholic church when I was 20 years old and later divorced. At 28 I met Mr. Right. He had never been married before. He was also Catholic. Our problem was that I had never gotten an annulment from the church for my first marriage. In order to be married in the church, I would have had to mill through a stack of paperwork and counseling sessions, supply witnesses, wait for a period of six months, and pay an annulment fee of $600. Instead, we ran away to Las Vegas and got married within 24 hours. We said "I do" at a religious service conducted by a woman minister at a quaint little white chapel.

PRENUPTIAL COUNSELING A SURVEY OF MAJOR RELIGIONS

The major religious denominations listed below suggest couples participate in premarital counseling before having a ceremony in their facility. The purpose is to ensure that couples will have the best possible chance at a successful marriage.

(CONTINUED)

As an expert who prides herself on having her finger on the pulse of the wedding industry, I must tell all brides about America's newest nuptial craze—the Getaway Wedding. Unlike the "runaway" type, guests—usually no more than 20—are invited and formal announcements are sent out. Brides bring their own gowns, but everything else is supplied by the hotel or wedding facility in such places as Las Vegas, Lake Tahoe, Florida, Hawaii, Jamaica, and the Virgin Islands. The couple is married in either a civil or religious service, and then stays for their honeymoon while guests depart after a most exciting weekend wedding adventure. The best part of all? This exciting, romantic happening is about one-third the cost of the average hometown wedding for 200 guests.

Jill, of Beckley, West Virginia, details the problems that parental pressures can cause.

There were so many pressures, especially from our parents, that we opted for a civil ceremony to avoid all the religious questions. Neither set of parents would actually say they objected to our getting married in the other's church, but we were aware of their discomfort. Although we really wanted a church wedding with all the trimmings, we also wanted to maintain the peace. After all, the ceremony is only 20 minutes long, and we were just as married either way. What we were surprised to learn was that Unitarian churches will perform a memorable ceremony in the church itself without any religious influence. So that's what we chose.

Local marriage counselors and societies and fellows related through the National American Ethical Union can also give you suggestions. Call the Union at 212-874-5210 for advice.

Donna, of Tempe, Arizona, offers another ceremony solution for divorced people.

Both my husband and I are divorced. He had gotten an annulment from his first marriage, but I did not have any church affiliation. We decided to call several churches and found that many permit wedding ceremonies for nonmembers but *all* have some kind of prenuptial class requirements and limits. I'm so glad we took the time to investigate this, especially because a church

---

Baptist: Four one-hour premarriage sessions are optional. This denomination has very strict rules about divorce and pregnant brides. Couples must consult individual churches for program details.

Catholic: Premarital program can consist of several personal interviews and a weekend retreat. Program usually begins four months before the ceremony.

Episcopalian: The engaged couples must be baptized Christians. Attendance at three counseling sessions is suggested. Program usually begins one month before the ceremony.

Jewish: Guidelines ask couples to attend three counseling sessions. Program usually begins two months before the ceremony.

Lutheran: Many premarriage programs exist because each congregation has its own requirements. Attendance at three to ten sessions is suggested. Program usually begins three months before the ceremony.

wedding made my marriage official in the eyes of my children from my former marriage.

The ceremony is the most important part of your wedding day. Officially before God, man, and the state, you become husband and wife. Whether it is strictly traditional or wildly unique, the ceremony at which you and your groom say "I do" should be an event you anticipate with great excitement because you've planned and rehearsed it with great care.

CHAPTER 4

The Reception

RECEPTION FACTS TO KNOW

Before You Decide:
1. Shop and Compare (At Least Three Reception Sites).
2. Meet With the Hall Manager in Person.
3. Take a Guided Tour of the Premises.
4. Discuss
   - Kinds of Receptions Offered
   - Room Capacity
   - Rental Fee—Overtime Charges
   - Parking
   - Bartenders
   - Refreshment Selections
   - Catering Restrictions
   - Serving Policies
   - Dance Facilities
   - Decorations

After You Decide:
1. Request an *Itemized* Contract.
2. Read the Contract Carefully.
3. Pay Only a 10 to 15 Percent Deposit.
4. Arrange a Payment Schedule in Writing.

The reception accounts for more than 35 percent, the biggest expense of your total wedding cost. Here you are, a young woman with no real party planning experience, planning the biggest party of your life. This chapter contains a lot of dos and, even more important, don'ts you will want to know about before you sign on any bottom line.

Large facilities, such as hotels, specialize in accommodations for perfect parties. Frequently all of their available party rooms are booked on the same day.

Ashley, of Washington, D.C., found crowds to be a real problem.

If I could, I would hold my reception in a place with only one hall. We rented in a place with three different halls hosting weddings. Perhaps our buffet was the most appetizing, because people wandered in from the other weddings and stepped into our food line with our guests. The embarrassing removal of these "crashers" almost ruined my wedding celebration.

Although hotels pride themselves on service and do everything possible to see that each party runs smoothly, unexpected things can happen. If you want "undivided attention," concentrate on single-hall facilities only! If you want the glamour of a hotel setting, understand that you are not the only customer.

A big formal wedding is the American bride's ultimate dream. With it comes the etiquette and protocol that makes it the grand affair that it is. But this is also your wedding, and it should be the kind of affair that you want.

Here is a list of other possible reception locations.

Aquariums	Ferryboats	Mountaintops
Art galleries	Grand ballrooms	Museums
Bed & breakfast	Hot air balloons	Nightclubs
inns	Hotels	Parks
Beach pavilions	Inns	Patios
Castles	Libraries	Public gardens
Catering halls	Lighthouses	Restaurants
Country clubs	Lofts	Sailboats
Civic centers	Mansions	Secluded beaches
Discos	Meeting halls	Sculpture gardens

WORLD'S MOST
EXPENSIVE WEDDING

The wedding of Mohammed, son of Sheik Rashid Bin Saeed Al Maktoun, to Princess Salema was held in Dubai in a specially constructed stadium for 20,000 guests, in May 1981. It lasted seven days and cost an estimated $22 billion.
—Guinness Book of World Records

Ski lodges	Terraces	Wineries
Sports arenas	Town houses	Yachts
Supper clubs	Trains	Yacht clubs
Taverns	Trolleys	Zoos
Tents	University campuses	

Susan, of Rochester, New York, recalls her big wedding disappointment.

Forget the big showy wedding! I would have had a smaller affair with less protocol. My mother made such a big deal about little things like "place cards." It was positively nerve racking, and really wasn't worth the hassle.

If you choose to have a formal wedding, eliminate hassles by developing a list of "to dos." Organize by delegating tasks to eager parents, relatives, and friends. They will feel as if their input is valued even if their ideas are not strictly adhered to.

Some brides want less, while others want more for their wedding receptions, as Donna, of Princeton, points out.

I regret that we didn't have a longer reception. We wanted a small affair with relatives and close friends. It seemed that the party had just gotten going when we ran out of time and had to leave the hall.

A wedding reception can range from a two-hour cake-and-cocktails-only reception, to a six-hour "party" that includes a champagne hour, a meal served (which accounts for another hour), and musical entertainment with dancing (four hours average).

Tracy, of Phoenix, advises brides to avoid being rushed and to enjoy every moment of their wedding day.

I'm sorry that we didn't set aside a room in the hotel after the ceremony just for my husband and myself so we could spend a short "special time" alone together to relax, enjoy a champagne toast together, and prepare to greet our guests at the reception. It seems that after all that time spent planning, the actual day is a rushed flurry of excitement that ends very quickly.

BRIDAL BARGAIN

A hotel can offer you several advantages, including discounted rates for out-of-town guest rooms and a free honeymoon suite on your wedding night. Don't be afraid to ask for special rates and other discounts that may be available to you. Hotels want to keep your business.

A great wedding is always well organized. Kelly, of Baltimore, made special plans for the children who attended her reception.

Will there be children at your reception? Consider hiring someone to entertain them, so their parents can enjoy the festivities more fully. Provide a table in a far corner equipped with crayons, coloring books, and storybooks to amuse small guests. Often children find waiting for a meal intolerable, so have treats on hand to ward off their hunger.

Patrice, of Tallahassee, asks, "How would you have liked a wedding that turned out backward?"

My whole wedding was topsy-turvy! To begin with, my groom and his attendants were in a car accident on the way to the chapel. Fortunately, no one was injured, but the group was detained until the police arrived and filled out the accident reports. Because of this, we could not be married until later that day because another wedding was scheduled in the chapel. However, the church hall and food were ready so we proceeded to hold our reception party before our ceremony. As guests arrived and congratulated us, we had to tell them "We're not married yet."

The only requirements for a wedding reception are a cake and a beverage for toasting the wedding couple. Champagne is the traditional beverage served at formal receptions. Many facilities offer "tastings" to bridal couples and their parents in order to select special champagnes or wines for their toasts. Refreshments are promoted because liquor is the biggest profit area for the party facilities.

Darlene, of Cleveland, cautions couples that refreshments are ordered on an estimated basis, which usually involves a "corking fee."

Our wedding reception was held at a country club. My mother was very concerned because the bartenders seemed to be pushing liquor on the guests. This really alarmed me because we were paying a "corking fee"—a charge for every bottle that was opened—whether or not they were poured! At $20 per bottle, my

---

BRIDE BEWARE

Reception sites either require the use of their in-house caterer or allow an off-site caterer to come in. Usually there is no "room charge" with an in-house caterer. However, some reception sites will also charge a separate room rental fee.

liquor bill accounted for more than 60 percent of my total reception costs.

*Most party facilities such as hotels, halls, and country clubs
require that you purchase their liquor for your party at their facility.
A markup on the liquor they serve is standard. Usually their house
brands are the most affordable, but they do not have the same taste
or quality. One way of controlling your costs is to give the caterer
a bottle limit. Ask the bartender to confer with you before he/she
goes beyond that amount.*

**Sally, of Bowling Green, Ohio, offers some excellent ideas
that are being implemented around the country.**

Today, much attention is given to what is seen as an over-
indulgence in alcoholic beverages. In addition, both our families
have strict religious scruples about alcohol. Because of these things,
we were very sensitive to this issue. We specified that no liquor was
to be used in the preparation of our food. As a courtesy to our
guests, we did serve beer, and also offered nonalcoholic drinks at a
separate bar. These included natural sodas and designer waters.
We not only appeased our families, but also restrained alcoholic
consumption by eliminating the offering of all hard liquor.

**Beverly, of Springfield, Illinois, passes on a reliable formula
for ordering refreshments.**

Our recently married friends gave us a good formula to use
to make sure that the drinks last as long as the festivities and to
determine the amount of refreshments you will need for your
wedding. They said to count on each guest having two drinks the
first hour and one more every hour after that. The later in the day
that the reception is held, the more guests generally will drink.

*Speaking of formulas, here's the protocol for toasting. One
stands to make a toast, rises to drink one, but sits to receive one.*

**Carla, of Duluth, Minnesota, offers some clever ways to cut
costs and promote healthful refreshments.**

For our wedding reception, our coordinator suggested a
unique idea to save money on our reception costs. We had a
champagne toast and after dinner offered a "soft bar," which

included a selection of wine, beer, soda, mineral water, virgin daiquiris, and pina coladas. Our guests just loved it, and several friends copied it for their weddings.

Tina, of Charlotte, North Carolina, warns that some religious denominations and church banquet halls have rigid rules about dancing.

Our wedding reception was held in our church banquet hall. There was no dancing allowed but contrary to what most people may think, we had a terrific celebration. We played soft, romantic background music and used every bit of our two-hour reception to its fullest. We started with a brunch, complete with a toast. Following this we needed all the time left to catch up with the lives and interests of our seldom-seen relatives and dear friends. Our guests socialized with us and each other and really enjoyed our wedding celebration.

Your wedding should be like a reunion of family and old friends, during which they enjoy every traditional part of your wedding with you (cake cutting, bouquet toss) as well as renew old ties.

Monica, of Newport Beach, California, illustrates the importance of reading your contract and getting everything in writing.

It's those little "extras" that make the wedding so wonderfully right! What they don't tell you is that it's those little "extras" that "break the bank." We planned an October wedding at a posh hotel. Many "extras" were suggested when we met with the hotel manager. A thing like coat checking was an extra $2 per person. With 210 guests, that would mean an extra $420. He also suggested that we hold our cocktail hour in the atrium around the swimming pool. No "extra" cost was mentioned, nor did we ask if there would be one. We decided that champagne would be served for our wedding toast. Our contract stated that each guest would receive one glass. We arranged to have the balance of our total bill, with any "extra" charges, sent to my parents' home following the wedding. That is much better than having to "settle up" the bill at the end of a long, exhausting day. When the bill arrived,

---

BRIDES' GREATEST FEARS ABOUT THE WEDDING DAY

1. The groom will not show up.
2. I won't have enough money for all the things I want to include.
3. I'll be so nervous that I'll gain 20 pounds and not fit into my wedding gown.
4. My long-distance wedding planning will turn out to be disastrous.
5. I'll cry throughout the entire ceremony.
6. We'll miss our plane for our honeymoon.
7. The weather will be bad.
8. I'll trip on my gown as I walk down the aisle.
9. My husband will faint at the altar.
10. I'll have to go to the bathroom during the ceremony.
11. Someone will stand up at the ceremony to oppose the marriage.
12. The food won't be good, or we'll run out of it.

the expected balance of approximately $1,000 had grown to an "extra" $3,000. The final bill stated that champagne was served, among other things, all night—extra cost $500. The "extra" cost for the tropical pool area was $500, and we didn't even swim! We were very disappointed.

People forget what was discussed months earlier. Put every detail in writing. If it is not written down, you should not be charged for it. And if it is written down, the cost should be written down too. Be sure to also scrutinize the wording of the contract. Words such as "made available" do not mean the same as "will be served." Ask to take the contract home with you so that you (and your parents) can read it over carefully.

While the basic requirement for a wedding reception are a wedding cake and a beverage for the bridal toast, don't forget atmosphere and comfort. Your reception site should be as elegant or as cozy as your wedding style, formal or informal. If you are planning a summertime affair, be sure that the site is fully air-conditioned.

CHAPTER 5

The Caterer

CATERING FACTS TO KNOW

Before You Decide:
1. Shop and Compare (At Least Three Caterers).
2. Personally Meet with Each Caterer.
3. Take a Guided Tour of Their Facilities.
4. Ask to See Previous Wedding Photos.
5. Discuss:
   • Menu choices and prices
   • Servers and gratuity fees
   • All service policies
6. Arrange for a "Tasting" at One of Their Upcoming Weddings.

After You Decide:
1. Read the Contract Carefully.
2. Pay Up to 25 Percent Initial Deposit.
3. Put "Everything" in Writing.
   • Include a payment schedule
   • Include a cancellation clause
4. Set a Date to Notify Caterer of Final Guest Count.

The wedding meal is the centerpiece of the reception. It visually reflects your good taste and your desire to treat your guests royally. It is also the number-one item guests will compliment or complain about. A fabulous feast can be provided in many ways. The key is to hire a competent caterer who will spend time with you describing all the options and explaining all of the terms.

Food is the most expensive item of the wedding celebration. Every bride wants her wedding to be fabulous, but sometimes appearances can be deceiving, as Leslie, of Oak Park, Illinois, discovered.

I was infatuated with an elegant restaurant that overlooked a beautiful lake setting. This facility had a great reputation, and I thought it would be the ideal setting for my reception. My fiancé and I went there and got a grand tour. The manager was very pleasant. He explained their policies and menu selections. He showed us photos of meal displays from past weddings. He even provided us with a complimentary taste of their best dessert and coffee. We booked our wedding there and then. On the wedding day itself, we were disappointed to discover the flaws we never saw. Our food was nothing like we had seen in the photos. And the quality was just so-so. There were not enough waitresses to serve our group, and they were extremely slow. To say the least, we were very disappointed. The service for our big party was totally different from the restaurant service we had experienced there in the past.

If you are considering a restaurant for your reception site, be sure to arrange a visit during another large party so that you can taste the food that has been prepared for that group. Sometimes busy facilities will use frozen foods that they purchase in bulk quantities. This is especially true of hors d'oeuvres and finger foods. Usually facilities "staff up" for large parties, but at times they also have to stretch their help. The standard rule is: One server per ten guests for a sit-down dinner, and one server for every main dish at the buffet. Also remember to ask for references. Call them. *After all, an inquiring bride has the right to know.*

A wedding is a very expensive party. Getting a signed contract with everything spelled out in writing should be for your benefit and protection. Diane, of Raleigh, North Carolina, learned that the hard way.

I was a bride with an unusual circumstance. My wedding was all planned and my fiancé was called to active duty in the Persian Gulf. Because we wanted a formal celebration, my entire wedding had to be postponed and rescheduled for a new date. My catering contract had an "escalator" clause. This gives the caterer the right to increase the fee per plate at their discretion. My caterer said that because of the rising costs of food and help, the price of my buffet dinner would rise 10 percent. I had already paid half of the anticipated cost, so there wasn't much that I could do. I advise everyone to read the contract carefully!

Careful reading is required, especially the fine print. Be sure to ask for an explanation of anything you do not understand. You have a right to do this. After all, it is your money that is paying for this party. Contracts vary throughout the country, but typically terms such as "escalator" and "overtime" mean services that cost more. If the facility offers an "all-inclusive" service, find out exactly what that means. Always be sure to compare their "package deal" prices to their regular à la carte menu. Sometimes the latter is really less expensive.

By getting everything in writing, Michelle, of Clearwater, Florida, resolved a very sticky situation.

I really liked my caterer. His enthusiasm and excellent reputation made me feel very comfortable. I worked hand in hand with him to select menu items that would impress and please my family of good cooks. The food was everything he promised. It looked like a picture, and tasted even better. Then I got the bill. It was $1,400 *over* the amount that had been indicated in my catering contract. On top of the gratuity fee that would be added, I was charged extra for the ice carvings, wages for the food station attendants, and a fee for cutting the cake. Thank goodness I had kept a copy of the original document—it was my evidence that decided this matter in my favor.

BRIDE BEWARE

An additional 15 to 20 percent gratuity fee is usually added to the total food and, sometimes, even the beverage bill. For example, you were quoted a $10 per person charge for your 200 guest meals. Your bill will be $2,000 plus the 20 percent "tip" of $400, which brings the grand total to $2,400.

Kristin, of Topeka, Kansas, who really "did her own thing," said:

If I could do it over again I would change my entire wedding. Mine was a real "do-it-yourself" affair. I baked my own wedding cake, prepared my own food, catered the reception party, made my own wedding bouquet—everything! Sure I saved a lot of money, but my wedding was more work than fun. And that's how I will always remember it.

If your wedding budget is limited, don't be afraid to ask for help from the friends and family (including your bridesmaids) who not only love you but are almost as excited about your wedding as you are. These people would be happy to contribute their time and talents to make your wedding great! By delegating jobs to qualified helpers (example: Aunt Bette, the gourmet cook, would probably love to be in charge of the wedding meal), you will free yourself of the task and be able to concentrate on the fun of organizing the wedding.

Jesse, of Guthrie, North Dakota, would like you to know that you have the right to verify your guest count.

I regret that I did not call the people who did not respond to their invitation to our reception dinner. Instead, I included 18 more names than I'd heard from in the final food count, and none of them showed up. Not only was it a waste of money, but the tables had to be cramped together in order to accommodate everyone. The entire room of tables would have been more elegant and more spacious if not for this.

When inviting people to a party, it is safe to estimate that one-fourth of them will not be able to attend. It is also proper for you, the bride, or someone in your family to call anyone who was sent a reception invitation and has not replied within three weeks. Invitations can be lost or misplaced, so it is wise to double-check. Usually the final count and the balance are not due to the caterer until the week before the wedding.

If you are working with a limited budget but want a formal, elegant affair, Karen, of Quincy, Oregon, offers her solution.

My fiancé and I wanted an elegant hotel wedding but our guest list totaled 200 and we absolutely could not afford to provide a meal for that many people. Our caterer at the hotel gave us a great idea. We arranged to be married at 2:00 in the afternoon and, immediately following, we held a two-hour champagne reception at which we served hot and cold hors d'oeuvres and wedding cake as dessert. The caterer suggested ten hors d'oeuvres per person, which were displayed on a large buffet table and looked appetizing and plentiful. We were very satisfied because we impressed our guests with this delicious variety of finger foods and still stayed within our budget.

The best advice I can give about hiring a caterer is to find one you feel you can trust. Hotel professionals pride themselves on "catering" to a bride's every need.

The wedding meal can be a bountiful buffet from which your guests serve themselves, or it can be a sit-down dinner during which they are served.

Robin, of Brentwood, Pennsylvania, shares more helpful information.

I knew that I wanted a formal wedding reception with a complete sit-down dinner. I didn't know that there are different kinds of sit-down service. One kind is called "French service." When guests arrive, they find tables that are completely set and a "starter" fruit cup or other appetizer is on each plate. The servers wheel a cart to each table and serve the rest of the meal "tableside," giving the guests individualized portions and attention. "Plate service," on the other hand, means that places are set at each table, but the plates are all prepared in the kitchen and brought out and served. The prep time and serving time is faster with this service, and it also costs less.

Heather, of Macon, Georgia, had an experience with a catering manager that proves how important organization really is.

We made an unfortunate mistake. Each family thought that the other had taken care of the balance of our bill, and everyone left the hotel. The next morning, as my husband and I were leaving, the catering manager ran out after us and practically tackled us in the lobby. It was very embarrassing.

Typically, facilities that feature weddings will require that both the food and the estimated bar bill be paid in full no later than 72 hours before the wedding. If all of the refreshments are consumed during the reception, the manager will notify whoever is paying the bill of the situation and decide with them how much more should be served. The bill for the excess is either presented at the end of the reception, or it is mailed the following day. All payment arrangements can be specified in the contract prior to the wedding day, specifically so the parties concerned can be prepared. In this way, there are no surprises or embarrassing situations.

If you want to learn how Glenda, of Austin, saved money on the catering charges, read on.

Our food was prepared by an independent caterer. The quality and quantity of the food was great. The service was superb. Most impressive to us was the way we were charged. Instead of the usual 20 percent gratuity fee (the service charge, or "tip," that is automatically added to the total food cost), we were charged an hourly rate per server. Specifically, our bill of $4,000 would normally have an $800 gratuity fee added to it. But we were charged $15 per hour for each of our six servers who worked at our four-hour reception. We paid a total service fee of $360 and saved $440.

While some brides share their stories of savings, Eileen, of Alexandria, Virginia, provides a valuable lesson learned through her losses.

I should have known that things were not very organized. The wedding hall we wanted had a kitchen but used outside caterers. The hall manager gave us a list of recommended companies. From the very start, I called and had to leave several messages before the owner called back to set up an appointment. Once we met, everything seemed in order and we did get a written contract. On our wedding day, the caterers and our meal arrived late. The owner never showed up. Despite the delay, the food was good and we were satisfied. The big surprise came after the wedding, when we attempted to get our security deposit back from the reception hall. The catering workers had left the kitchen in a total mess, and the hall manager's wife spent all day cleaning it before another

WEDDING LORE

Wedding weather has always had significant meaning. Sunshine on the wedding day brought luck, snow foretold of riches, while rain was a sign of tears.

party the next evening. We had no provision about clean-up with the caterer, so our $100 deposit was "swept" away.

It is standard procedure that a rental hall requires a security deposit to cover any damage that the renter or their guests may cause. The contracts also say that the party who is renting the hall is responsible for removing decorations and returning the hall to its original condition. If you are using a hall for your reception party, be sure to clarify clean-up conditions with your caterer and arrange for a cleaning crew of family members or friends to remove the bells and streamers.

As with all things, there are caterers and there are caterers. Shannon, of Westport, Connecticut, tells of one who went beyond the call of duty in the service he provided for her wedding.

I want other brides to know about a very sweet and thoughtful thing that our caterer did for us. Like most wedding couples, we were very busy visiting with our guests and posing for candids. It was all very exciting, but we did not eat much of our wedding meal. Near the end of the reception, the caterer presented us with a beautiful wicker basket filled with samples from our buffet. Included were two pieces of wedding cake with extra frosting (my husband has a big sweet tooth). It was delicious and greatly appreciated by two people who, by that evening, were very hungry!

According to Pam, of Tacoma, Washington, an ideal caterer is honest, reliable, helpful and comes highly recommended, like this one.

Finding a good affordable caterer was one of our greatest challenges. Great caterers do not always have the biggest ads, so we decided to not let our fingers do all the walking. Instead, we trusted "word of mouth" recommendations and got the best! My cousin recommended this woman who runs a catering business out of her home. She has a small, dedicated crew that has worked for her for over ten years, and she only takes on so many parties per month. She didn't have a big fancy office, but she had all of the elegant serving pieces, ice carvings, and a knack for serving mouth-watering displays of scrumptious food. She showed us photos of past parties. She invited us to attend a function she was doing to taste her food and see her service. We had a written catering order and it was followed to the "T." The best part about her was the time and care she took to help us stretch a limited budget. She suggested that we schedule a late-morning wedding ceremony and follow it with a luncheon reception. Not only were we pleased with the bountiful buffet that was served, but we spent 30 percent less than we thought we would have to.

Most brides dream about their wedding day. Stephanie, of Hancock, Vermont, relives her wedding nightmare.

It began as I was walking down the aisle. I looked down and saw that my flower girl was scattering polystyrene packaging "peanuts" instead of rose petals. As I glanced quickly toward the altar, I saw my entire wedding party standing and eating hamburgers. The pastor beckoned me to come forward. When I did, I saw his gigantic shoes and bright red hair. It was none other than Ronald McDonald!

Stephanie was terrified that her dream was an omen about her caterer. Her mother put her arms around Stephanie and replied, "Sweetheart, you just have a good case of wedding jitters."

Regardless of where your reception is held, the one comment you will enjoy hearing after the wedding is "We really had a great time—the food was fabulous." If you want your food and service to be memorable and special, take the utmost care in choosing the right caterer.

CHAPTER 6

The Photographer/Video

THE PHOTOGRAPHER/VIDEO
FACTS TO KNOW

1. Use a Photographer Whose Equipment and Experience Qualify Him or Her as a Wedding Professional.
2. Photographers Can Be Booked One Year in Advance. Expect to Pay a Deposit of One-third to One-half When the Booking Is Contracted.
3. Sample Books of Previous Weddings Should Be Available to See the Quality of the Photographer's Work.
4. Photographers Offer Their Services on an Hourly Basis or Through a "Packaged" Agreement.
5. Photography Packages Can Range from $300 to $2,500. The Average Couple Spends Approximately $750 to $1,000 for Their Wedding Photographs.
6. The Photography Contract Should Detail All Expectations Including Special Photographs Required.
7. Today 60 to 80 Percent of All Weddings Are Videotaped.
8. There Are Several "Styles" of Wedding Videos That Can Tell Your Wedding Story.
9. Shop and Compare for Quality and Price.
10. Demonstration Tapes of Other Weddings Should Be Available for Your Viewing.
11. Ceremony Locations and Any Videotaping Restrictions Must Be Discussed and Planned For.
12. Professional Photographers and Videographers Should Carry Full Liability Insurance Coverage.
13. Today a Complete Video Wedding Story Can Be Purchased. This Includes Taping of the Bridal Shower, Bachelor Party, and Rehearsal Dinner as Well as the Wedding Day.

Next to your wedding itself, wedding photographs are often regarded as the longest lasting memory you will have of your wedding. The importance of hiring a professional to record this one-take-only event cannot be stressed enough. Brides need to know the basic facts and also to be aware of the photography/video "scams" that exist. The information included in this chapter tells how brides have dealt with large studios and how they handled wedding day disappointments. This information can prevent a real wedding day disaster while, at the same time, showing you how to select a quality photographer.

Today wedding photography and videos are more formal, more old-fashioned, and more romantic. Brides want their albums to look more like their grandmother's than their mother's.

Joan, of Durham, North Carolina, expressed this idea well.

I love the Victorian era. I selected a tea-length dress with ivory lace and ribbon trim. My photographer created an old-fashioned storybook with vignette poses with darkened edges and some of those rigid formal poses of family groups. The elegant ornate restaurant at which our reception dinner party was held made the background setting perfect.

Some photographers mix tradition with modern special effects, according to Sharon, of Marion, Ohio.

My photographer was a real cut-up. He brought along a bag of rubber clown noses. He posed our entire bridal group in a rigid old-fashioned pose with everyone wearing a red nose. This "trick shot" was the most talked-about photo in our album.

Other trick shots include a silhouette pose of a bridal couple positioned in a keyhole frame and a photograph of a couple dancing their first dance while superimposed on a piece of sheet music with the title of "their song" at the top.

Claudia, of Lawton, Oklahoma, has a clever idea for picture lovers.

We love pictures, and we wanted to capture every moment of this special time in our life. So to accomplish this, we made picture taking an important part of our reception party by passing out disposable cameras to guests as they arrived. They snapped away all evening and then, after putting their name on the box, placed them in a large container as they left. We placed one or two photos in each thank-you note we sent and kept the rest. Some of the candids are priceless.

Another couple, who had just bought their first home, had the photographer go out there to take photos of the groom carrying the bride over their very own threshold.

Statistical Facts:
- 80 percent of America's wedding couples blame the photographer for the troubles at their wedding.
- 76 percent would never hire the same photographer again.
- 85 percent of brides arrive late for their photographs.

It is also important that couples know a wedding album keeps photos from fading.

Ron, of Newark, was a groom who got into the picture too.

Typically you'll see pictures of the bride and her maids getting dressed at the bride's home, but my husband wanted to be in the picture too. To accomplish this, the photographer went to his home too and got some darling comic shots of him shaving with only his white bow-tie on, and another with the best man and his dad hurrying him out of the door with one of his shirt tails still untucked. They showed both of us preparing for our big event.

Natalie, of Concord, New Hampshire, captured generations of good luck at her wedding.

We have the good fortune of being a part of a hearty, healthy family. We have several four generation groupings among our relatives. In order to capture these precious photos, we appointed a responsible cousin to gather together and aid our photographer for special shots like these and other important ethnic traditions that we wanted photographed. It was great to know that nothing would be missed and we would be able to cherish these moments forever.

Wedding photographs are a slice of family history that will bring more and more joy to you and your loved ones as your anniversaries roll by.

BRIDAL BARGAIN

Purchase a photo album at a local stationery or department store. Create your own personalized picture story of your wedding.

Good wedding photographers:
1. Enjoy their art and are fun to be with.
2. Know their equipment and special techniques.
3. Have creative vision and an eye for details.
4. Are excellent organizers.

Brenda, of New Rochelle, New York, tells how her photographer became her wedding referee.

Both of the fathers in our families are big feisty men—even when they're sober. They started arguing with my caterer, and my photographer tried to get between them to settle it quietly. Instead, the argument escalated into chair throwing and punches. That's when the photographer decided to just duck and huddle to guard his equipment. My photographer ended up being the only sober witness to testify in court. I spent the night driving my mother home, while my new husband and my new father-in-law spent the night in jail. If it had not been for the photographer, we would have had to pay for poor service as well as the damaged party room. I only wish that he would have been able to take one picture to show these men how they ruined my wedding day.

The average wedding party of the '90s includes a minimum of five bridesmaids.

Here's an idea on how one photographer handles these large groups.

My fiancé and I wanted a big wedding party. We had so many close relatives and friends that we could not eliminate anyone. Our bridal party consisted of 14 couples. Our photographer took some clever group shots. First, all of the "relatives" in our bridal party were photographed together as a group. Then he posed all of our "friend" members together in a different group setting. Everyone got into the picture, and these special photos made it easy for us to use them as a unique remembrance gift.

A video may be a moving memory, but you can't hang it over the mantel to look at each time you enter the room. Vivian, of St. Paul, Minnesota, tells how she "adapted" her wedding portrait.

We purchased a beautiful 20 by 30, $350, full-length oil portrait of ourselves on our wedding day. Today, six months later, I am divorced. The portrait hangs in my living room displayed on a prominent wall with my ex-husband's full head cut out of the picture. It gives me great comfort to never have to see his face again.

Then there's the story of the bride who said "If a picture is worth a thousand words, my wedding will be an epic novel."

It is a wise idea to call the Better Business Bureau to check out all records of complaints against any wedding firm you are doing business with *before* you hire it, warns Dina, of Portsmouth, Virginia.

I hired a photographer based on portraits that he had displayed at a local bridal fair. My wedding was in April. In June I was told my proofs were ready. They were a big disappointment. The few I did want, I asked to be ready for Christmas presents. They argued that it took six months to process the finished prints. They never did arrive. In February my husband started calling. By our first anniversary, the promised albums were received but had to be returned because the dates on the covers were wrong.

Dates for proof arrivals and album completion are musts, in writing, on all photography contracts. Special points can even be written in by hand, as long as the document is signed by both parties.

If you have had an unjustly managed business encounter, don't be afraid to write a letter of complaint to the Better Business Bureau of your city. If at least 20 complaints are lodged against a firm, it can be reported to the state attorney general's office for a pattern of fraudulent behavior.

BRIDE BEWARE

Be aware that a sales tax is added to the total cost of the photographer's bill. Make sure your grand total is listed.

Peggy, of South Bend, Indiana, reports on this.

If I could redo one thing about my wedding, I would have selected a different photographer. We went to one of the most reputable studios in the area, expecting to get a top-notch professional to photograph our wedding story. We were assured that all of their photographers were very well trained. Unfortunately, our photographs reflected just how inexperienced the man behind our camera was.

It is your prerogative to require that the name of your particular photographer or videographer be included on your contract. You also have the right to meet this person and see samples of his/ her work before you sign anything. If the studio will not do this, I suggest you continue shopping.

A good guideline for selecting your photographer or videographer is—if the person has successfully completed 20 weddings, you can trust that he/she is the experienced pro you are seeking.

Pauline, of Decatur, Illinois, offers some helpful tips.

Many photographers in our city offer wedding packages. They were all fairly competitive and explained to us that "packages" varied according to (1) the amount of shooting time the photographer would be needed and (2) the number and sizes of the prints that would be included. We really appreciated having this explained to us because it made it very simple for us, knowing that we would get all of the traditional photos we wanted taken by a professional. Most of all, we knew exactly what the total cost would be, and we could budget properly for it.

Be sure that the package you select provides an adequate selection. The average wedding album usually uses 60 to 80 prints to tell a complete wedding story.

Camille, of Orlando, thought she had a real bridal bargain.

We got a great photography bargain. Our photographer offered us a package that included 20 8 by 10s for one low sum. It was just great!

Low-price packages are fine, but also remember that after 20, each additional photo is considered a "reprint" and is more costly. Because photographers snap as many as 100 shots throughout a wedding, it sometimes becomes very difficult to limit the total number you want to just 20.

Beware of a photographer who says that he/she can accomplish a style you desire, such as "soft-focus" pictures, when the sample books you are shown have no examples like that.

Wedding photography does not always have to be a "package" deal, explains Barb, of Knoxville, Tennessee.

A well-known and creative photographer in our city offers his customers a "menu" of selections. We met with him and discussed the details of our wedding. We decided that we would need him for a three-hour time period. Thus, we paid him an hourly fee for that time. After the wedding, we looked at the proofs and selected only the ones we specifically wanted and paid a separate price for each. I feel that was the most practical and precise way of purchasing a customized wedding album.

No matter how your photographer sets up charges, the biggest concern for you, the buyer, is the total cost you will be responsible for. There are no standardized blanket prices for photographers because the most important thing you are buying is their creativity and experience.

Wedding photographs include two categories—wedding candids, which are spontaneous shots taken during the wedding day capturing its fun and excitement, and posed photographs taken at the ceremony site or some prearranged picturesque setting, often used for newspaper announcements or as keepsake mementos.

Marla, of Griffin, Georgia, offers some timesaving ideas about when the posed photographs should be taken.

Our caterer and our photographer suggested that we take our posed family portraits before the ceremony. By doing this, we avoided rushing and the fear of keeping our guests waiting at the reception. Because my mother-in-law felt it was unlucky for the groom to see the bride before the ceremony, we took separate photos with our families and bridal party members. In this way, we didn't disturb the superstition; yet we saved more than half the time it would have otherwise taken.

Posed picture sessions taken between the ceremony and the reception should definitely be limited warns Jenna, of Rutland, Vermont.

I am sorry that we did not allow more time between the ceremony and reception. Because we had our photographs taken right after the ceremony, we missed the entire cocktail hour. All we saw of it was from the video, and it looked great.

By no means is there any such thing as being fashionably late for your own wedding reception.

Alicia, of Ogden, Utah, shares her pre-wedding photography philosophy.

My husband and I discussed taking our photos before the ceremony. We thought that it made a lot of sense to take the photos when everyone was fresh. We also felt that it took the edge off feeling nervous. Most important, it gave us a special quiet time together to celebrate our relationship and to exchange gifts with each other. By doing this, we were able to concentrate on the ceremony and appreciate it more. And on top of it all, I still felt the thrill of my grand entrance and walk down the aisle in front of all of my relatives and friends.

A new product available is called a photographic thank-you card. The couple chooses one of their favorite posed photos. It is mass printed on the back of a postcard and can be used as a unique keepsake thank-you for all who attend their event.

Speaking of unique ideas, Jolene, of Flagstaff, Arizona, offers this one.

I created a unique item that has become as precious to us as our wedding photo album. I made a wedding memory scrapbook. Everything from my engagement party invitations to our wedding newspaper announcement and a final section on souvenirs from

---

WEDDING LORE

In 1775, colonial law stated that a young woman could not be married wearing any makeup. Makeup was considered a way to trap the groom by its illusion. The wedding, therefore, would not be legitimate.

our fabulous honeymoon documented all of the work and costs that made our day so magical.

A lot of talented women enjoy creating hand-crafted items that can be used as a remembrance of their wedding. Floral decorated place cards, fabric covered video-tape boxes, and framed invitations that include some of the flowers from their wedding bouquets are just a few of the many ideas that can be discovered at craft and variety stores across America.

If you are a bargain hunter, you can save money by:
- Hiring a photographer or a videographer for your ceremony *only*. You'll save about 50 percent.
- Using the talents of shutterbug friends and family, supply the disposable "film in the camera" cameras on all of the reception tables. Provide a "place camera here" drop-box at the reception room exit. This will allow for a great variety of candid shots, as it is impossible for one photographer to be everywhere at one time.
- It is not necessary to provide parents and grandparents with their own miniature album of your wedding. A framed portrait is sufficient.
- Using black and white film instead of color for cost savings as well as special effects. Special tints and lens filters can also create unusual effects at substantial savings.
- Making copies yourself of your original video, or calling companies listed in your local yellow pages under "audio/visual services" to check their costs for reproduction. The average runs $10 to $20 per tape.

Rosalyn, of Hot Springs, Arkansas, believes that while a photograph captures a single moment, a video is a moving memory.

My best advice to all brides is . . . have a wedding video. Don't get married without it. And most important, HIRE A PROFESSIONAL! It brings tears to our eyes to hear our vows again as we said them, and our song playing as we danced our first dance. We laugh every time we see the bridesmaids jumping up and grabbing for my wedding bouquet, and hear the hilarious toast our best man gave. We can relive all of it again and again as a moving memory of our once-in-a-lifetime event.

Each magic moment of your wedding day can be captured and electronically edited to produce a complete love story that starts from the moment you awaken until you wave goodbye as you drive away. I'd recommend this service to every bride.

Marcia, of Oakland, California, explains that professional video companies offer the latest equipment, wireless microphones, low-light cameras and the knowledge and skill that mark the difference between professional and neophyte.

A close family friend who is an aspiring video buff offered, as a gift, to videotape our wedding. He even rented the newest equipment and really worked hard throughout the day to capture every important moment of our celebration. The idea was wonderful, but the ½-inch VHS home tapes did not produce the superb visual quality we had hoped for, nor was he able to remove the distracting background sounds or the thousands of feet of cord needed for the lights that my grandfather tripped on. Secretly I was very disappointed that our big day was a linked series of stops and starts. **Your wedding is a one-shot deal. There can be no retakes like you see in the movies.** I learned the hard way. You get what you pay for. The average price for a video "package" is $500. This includes the actual taping and one finished master tape. Depending on the style of video that is chosen, the price can range from $100 to $2,000.

Nancy, of Waukegan, Illinois, created her very own "wedding movie."

My fiancé nearly drove me crazy with his new toy—a camcorder. Every event—the engagement party, showers, bachelor bash and rehearsal dinner (he actually had the waiter videotape us at the restaurant dinner table when we toasted with our champagne, and I found my diamond ring)—was captured on film. He even took it with us on our honeymoon. At times, it was nerve wracking, but it also turned out to be the most beautiful love story that I have ever seen. The professional videographer who shot our wedding took all of these other tapes and edited them together for us to create our own unique wedding movie.

The average wedding video shooting time is four hours. In that period, a professional videographer can capture all of the special, as well as the unplanned, excitement of your wedding day. Some brides add items to their basic videos to make them uniquely personal, such as:

- A collage of pictures that trace the childhoods of both the bride and groom.
- A personal message spoken by the bride and groom and recorded into the tape at a sentimental moment.
- Testimonials from family members and friends taken during the reception party.
- The inclusion of "their song" as background music played throughout the tape.
- Special techniques such as dissolves, split screens, or colorizations. Unique graphics with the couple's names, wedding date, or cartoon caricatures have also been used.
- Adding on footage or slides from the honeymoon completes the video to achieve a real "moving album" of your wedding experience.

You should spend no more than 10 percent of your total wedding budget on your wedding photography. Remember, the trick to excellent picture taking is the qualified eye behind the lens. Next to your lives together, your wedding photographs and video will last the longest.

The Wedding Party

PARTY MEMBERS FACTS TO KNOW

1. People Who Agree to Be Your Attendants Are Giving You Their Help, Their Time, and Their Financial Support.
2. Honor Attendants Must Be 21 Years of Age to Legally Witness and Sign the Marriage Certificate. Parents May Also Serve as Honor Attendants.
3. There Is No Limit to How Many Attendants You Can Have in Your Party.
4. The Head Usher Should Be Able to Recognize Most Guests.
5. The Ring Bearer May Be a Boy or a Girl.
6. It Is Customary to Give Attendants a Thank-you Gift.

On their special day, the bride and groom want to surround themselves with those people who are nearest and dearest to them. Accomplishing this task is not as easy as it appears. The experiences in this chapter describe the clever ideas couples used to choose the perfect people to be their wedding attendants and how they anticipated problems that arose among party members. Parents as attendants, problems with selecting and dealing with children as attendants, and handling last-minute changes are also featured.

It is always a problem to choose people especially when you have many close friends and relatives. Danielle, of Frankfort, Indiana, has a unique solution.

My fiancé and I were in a real jam. We had so many close friends that we didn't know whom to include in our wedding party. We got a brilliant idea. We had a prewedding barbecue and each person put his name in a white top hat. I drew the names of the three women who would be my bridesmaids. My husband followed by drawing the three men's names. After the names were announced, we all enjoyed a great afternoon. It definitely was a fun and fair way to choose.

Patti, of Harrison, Iowa, suggests a new escort idea for the '90s wedding.

I have read in etiquette books that a "man" escorts the bride down the aisle. If her father is deceased, a brother, uncle, or family friend may take his place. But, this is the '90s and women's liberation is a fact. My father is deceased. I do not have any brothers or uncles. My mother is totally responsible for my education and good upbringing, and she walked me down the aisle and gave me in marriage to my husband. Our entire family thought it was a unique and fitting idea.

In Jewish ceremonies both parents escort the bride and groom down the aisle. This custom is now being practiced in Christian ceremonies as well.

Vanessa, of Lebanon, Kentucky, suggests what to do when you no longer feel close to a bridesmaid.

About a year and a half ago, I asked a friend to be one of my bridesmaids. In the subsequent months, she complained about

> ### BRIDE BEWARE
>
> *The most common cause of friction between the bride and her bridesmaids is the style and color of the dresses. Any serious objections should be heeded. Forcing one's closest friends to wear clothes that they hate will bring nothing but trouble.*

the cost of the dresses and lost all interest in my plans. Because her parents and mine are close friends, I was afraid of causing ill will if I replaced her. We met for lunch and I explained my feelings and concern about the financial burden the wedding seemed to be causing her. She sighed with relief at being allowed to exit gracefully and left looking forward to being a guest at my wedding.

One word of advice. If the story ends happily as this one did, that's fine. However, if she does not volunteer to withdraw, it is neither correct nor courteous to ask her to.

Linda, of Monroe, Louisiana, tells about the quarrel between her mother and her honor attendant.

Although my honor attendant has two children and they live with their father, she is unmarried. She wants to be called "maid of honor" and my mother feels otherwise. The lady from whom we ordered our invitations felt that even though my friend's personal history was such, she still had never been married and would be considered a maid of honor.

A compromise solution would be to simply identify her as an honor attendant. In the '90s, few guests remember or care if a bridal attendant is a "maid" or a "matron."

Kim, of Frederick, Maryland, shares important tips about the "costs" of attendants.

Brides be warned! When you ask friends, especially those who live out of town, to be in your wedding party, you *are* responsible for some of their expenses. When I asked my old college roommate to be in my bridal party, I thought that when she accepted, she understood the time she would have to donate and the costs she would have to incur. Boy, was I wrong! My married sister-in-law quietly told me that while attendants buy their entire outfits and pay for their own travel expenses, their lodging while here was my responsibility.

Your sister-in-law provided good advice that I'm sure eliminated what could have been a real thorn in the side. You are responsible for paying for and providing a hotel room, your home, or a room at a relative's or friend's residence. You are also responsible for out-of-town attendants' transportation to and from airports, as well as to and from the locations involved in the wedding festivities.

Jodi, of Cambridge, Massachusetts, tells about her 100 wedding witnesses.

I am an only child and did not have a special friend who could be my honor attendant. Instead, all the guests who attended our wedding ceremony were witnesses to our marriage. My husband and I chose my grandmother and his grandfather as our official witnesses, and they legally signed our marriage license after the ceremony.

Debbie, of Columbus, Ohio, cautions brides about selecting their party members.

When I became engaged, I immediately started to pick out the members of my bridal party. I considered my future sister-in-law, but she is very overweight. She and I are not really close, so in order to avoid any confrontations over my conviction that she lose weight if she wanted to be in my wedding, I decided not to ask her at all. The wedding is over, but the hurt feelings aren't. I made a big mistake and started my new family relationship off on a sour note.

If you are worried that someone's appearance might detract from your bridal party, consider offering that person another opportunity to be a special participant in the festivities. Remember, the essence of a wedding is the uniting of two families.

Follow this wise advice from Liz, of Battle Creek, Michigan.

In all the excitement of getting engaged, I asked my future sister-in-law to be in my wedding. I only planned on one attendant. Then my family insisted that my cousin be in it, so I was faced with a real dilemma. I decided that I would expand my party and include both my cousin and my sister-in-law. I could not and would not hurt her feelings.

A wedding is primarily a family affair. By gathering your future in-laws around you, you are reaffirming that they are now your family too. This bride did the right thing.

WEDDING LORE

Age-old Roman customs dictated that ten witnesses were required to be present at a marriage ceremony. Their job, by their number, was to outwit the jealous demons whose purpose was to spoil the happy event in any way they could.

Amy, of Pueblo, Colorado, tells what to do with two "best" friends.

When we married we had two very close male friends and two very close female friends. The women problem was easily solved because one was married and the other was not. Thus, one served as my matron of honor and the other was the maid of honor. But you cannot have two best men. So what we did was solve the problem with a toss of a coin. One man served as best man; the other served as our head usher. He escorted both mothers down the aisle and drove us to the airport the next morning to see us off on our honeymoon. We bought both men and women the same gifts of thanks because they all had made an equally important contribution to our special day.

Kathleen, of Flint, Michigan, advises how attendants can add formality to your wedding.

I'm sorry that we didn't have our bridal party participate in the receiving line. They were scattered all around the church, and I wish we had thought to have them stand facing us in our receiving line. It would have given it a nice formal touch.

The receiving line is not held at the church unless the reception party is too. The "receiving line" is exactly what it says—the line of wedding members who receive the guests at their party. In other words, it is the welcoming committee at the reception, and bridesmaids, according to protocol, are supposed to be in that line.

Sandra, of Burlington, Vermont, shares some insight about the "little attendants."

Our pastor has been at our church for 20 years. During that time, he has officiated at many marriage ceremonies. Because of this, he set a new policy regarding children in the wedding party. The little attendants can be no younger than four years of age. Too many complications arise in ceremonies with younger children.

The best ages for flower girls or ring bearers is four to seven years. A ring bearer may be a boy or a girl. Junior bridesmaids range in age from ten to 16. In England, it is customary for the bride to have six "little attendants" in her party. If you have already promised your niece, age three, that she is going to be your flower girl, it would be wise to check with your clergy member or, if strict rules exist, investigate alternate sites for your ceremony.

Jacqueline, of Reading, Pennsylvania, suggests that you consider a "Handi Annie" for your wedding.

My niece is 13 and while I did not wish to have a junior bridesmaid in my party, my mother suggested I have her do a reading during the ceremony. She also became my "Handi Annie" and was there to address envelopes, make favors, and handle many other "little jobs" I did not have time for.

You show how much you care about someone when you let him or her share in the significant events of your life.

Tiffany, the six-year-old daughter of Dana, of Seattle, solved her mom's attendant problems by stating "Mom, I'll be your best woman."

Although men do not usually become intimately involved in the wedding planning, they can and do offer invaluable assistance in other ways. Diane, of Wheeling, West Virginia, tells about an "extraordinary" usher.

My husband's friend who was an usher in our wedding party really performed beyond the call of duty for us. When his brother was married last year, he served as his best man. He helped him save time by getting all the legal forms he and his wife needed for changing their names on bank accounts, driver's licenses, et cetera. He also delivered them when they were completed and did all of that for us too. It was a wonderful and helpful contribution.

This gracious performance should be copied across America.

Keith, of Evanston, Illinois, discusses his special best man.

I felt that the only man who was dearest, closest, knew me yet loved me in spite of it, was my dad—thus, my first choice for my best man.

It is perfectly proper for parents to be honor attendants. Relatives or friends can serve too, as long as they are 21 years old, so that they can legally witness and sign your marriage certificate.

Lynette, of St. Charles, Michigan, relates some wise fatherly advice.

My father, who was a perfect "gem" throughout the entire planning of our wedding, had a great saying about his role in the event. He said that he was told to "show up, shut up, and pay up." He also added that the memory was worth far more than the money.

These are endearing sentiments, and other fathers may well appreciate your dad's reassurances.

Marissa, of Davenport, Iowa, explains how her maid of honor was a man.

My best friend is male. I wanted him to be my honor attendant. He was willing and my fiancé had no objection. Our clergyman, who had done this before, helped us tremendously. My friend wore a tuxedo like the other groomsmen and walked in with the groom and the best man. He took a place on my side of the altar and waited for me to arrive there. It worked perfectly.

It is also possible to have your man of honor walk in the processional just after the ushers and wait in the same place that you described. Either is appropriate. Perhaps you can try both ways at the wedding rehearsal to see which is preferable.

Jan, of Omaha, explains how her best man almost "lost" it.

Our best man was so concerned about losing the ring that our pastor suggested he take it out of the velvet box and put it on his left index finger, somewhere between the knuckle and the nail. He assured him that it would be safe there as others had used this advice. He jammed the ring so tightly that it would never get lost or come off! After some unceremonious tugging, the ring finally gave way. It was amusing to watch as the beads of sweat ran down his temples. As a remembrance, we took a picture showing our hands with our rings—my husband's hand with his ring on holding my hand with my engagement ring only on, and the best man's hand over ours with my wedding ring on his little finger. Our photograph won a photo contest with it.

Scott, of Bay City, Michigan, discusses a lesson in good grooming.

I know that for the most part brides are telling the stories of their weddings, but as an "experienced" groom I learned a valuable lesson I would like to pass along. I had a best friend from my childhood and high school days. After high school, I received a naval scholarship to attend an out-of-state college. I met my fiancée while at college and we married this year. When I became engaged, I called my old friend and asked him to be in my wedding party. He gladly accepted and was very happy for me. During the planning time, I had ship duty and was gone a lot. The bottom line is, my fiancée and I neglected my friend. He called and called to find out what was happening. He even paid an extra fee to the tuxedo company because he had to be measured in another state. Two weeks before the wedding day, he called to ask about accommodations. My fiancée had contracted with the hotel for a block of rooms for our out-of-town guests, but he was not considered. I had to call him back to tell him that we had arranged hotel accommodations a mile down the road and that it would cost $70 per night. My friend called me back. He approached me honestly. He stated this concern about the haphazard way he had been treated and neglected. He felt that, under the circumstances, he did not wish to give three days of his time, $210 for a sleeping room, the balance of the tuxedo, and a wedding gift when little or no effort had been given to him as my friend. The truth is that my fiancée, who did not really know him, made no effort to make him feel included all the while I was on ship. He bowed out of the wedding and my wife's cousin quickly substituted. I didn't say anything because I feel that I was just as much to blame, as it was my friend, and my responsibility as the groom to keep in touch with him especially since he was out of state. We had a lovely wedding, but I must admit, I did miss my old friend's presence.

Not only did you neglect your friend, you mishandled your duty to provide a room for him, at your expense. If a hotel was too costly, perhaps your family home or another relative's house should have been arranged for him.

IF I COULD REDO ONE THING ABOUT MY WEDDING:

1. *I would have a nicer wedding gown.*
2. *I would not invite so many people.*
3. *I would have a church wedding instead of a garden wedding.*
4. *I would bring my family into town to be able to celebrate with me.*
5. *I would run away to an island to be married.*
6. *I would take more time for planning and budget more money.*
7. *I would have a smaller wedding.*
8. *I would have something unique and memorable to celebrate our day.*
9. *I would never have planned a long-distance wedding.*
10. *I would hire a bridal consultant.*
11. *I would not let other people's opinions influence my decisions.*

You choose your attendants because of your mutual love and friendship for each other. From the moment they accept your invitation to serve as members of your bridal party, treat them as a very special part of your special day. As long as you keep this positive spirit, everyone will perform his and her duties willingly and sincerely.

Wedding Attire

WEDDING ATTIRE FACTS TO KNOW

Bridal Gown:
1. Shop Six Months Before the Wedding for Your Gown.
2. The Veil and Headpiece Are *Separate* Items.
3. Ask About the Bridal Store's Exchange and Cancellation Policy.
4. Alterations Are an Extra Charge.
5. Put Everything in Writing, Including Delivery Date.
6. One-third Deposit Is Usually Required.
7. Keep All Receipts.

Groom's Attire:
1. The Groom May Wear a Different Color Tuxedo from the Groomsmen's.
2. The Groom May Wear a Business Suit at an Informal Wedding.
3. All Accessories, Including Shoes, Come with a Tuxedo Rental.

Attendants' Attire:
1. Bridesmaid Dresses Should Be No Longer Than the Bride's Gown.
2. Shoes Should Match or Coordinate with the Dresses.
3. Bridesmaid Dresses Do Not Have to Be Identical.
4. Junior Bridesmaid—Best Ages 10 to 16 Years Old.
5. Flower Girl/Ring Bearer—Best Ages Four to Nine Years Old.

A bride considers her wedding to be her very own formal pageant at which she will reign as "queen." Her most important purchase of the entire wedding is her wedding gown. Her greatest fear is that it will not arrive in time for her wedding. This chapter lists the things to know and the possibilities and problems related to the selecting, ordering, and altering of wedding attire. Also included are stories, and solutions, about problems connected with the ordering, fitting, and delivery of tuxedos.

Stacy, of Augusta, Minnesota, shares some smart shopping advice.

The best advice I received about buying my wedding gown was from my sister-in-law, who told me to shop for my dress during the week. Many bridal shops have evening hours. One shop did not and I attempted to go there on a Saturday. It was so crowded that people were waiting outside. I also learned, after I got there, that some shops require an appointment—so, to avoid any unnecessary trips, call ahead. Finally, don't take all of your bridesmaids with you—all it does is give you too many opinions. Besides, I was sorry that everyone saw my gown. It took away from my "grand entrance" on my wedding day.

Connie, of St. Petersburg, Florida, shares her insight about bridal salon facilities.

They say you never get a second chance to make a first impression. The bridal boutiques in my medium-size city ranged from elegant and palatial to "dirty" and out-of-date. I much preferred the smaller shop that had a cozier atmosphere. I also appreciated an individual fitting room. I did not like the pushy, pressured "hard sell" or the indifference I was shown after I told the sales clerk that I was planning to sew my bridesmaids' dresses myself. I also did not know that bridal salons stock and sell strapless bras and slips that really help for a proper fit. Some of the freebies I was offered with a purchase included free alterations, free pressing, free delivery of the gown to the church, with dressing assistance, and free pickup, cleaning, boxing, and return after the wedding. When I started shopping, I was looking for the best dress at the best price. But in reality, that was only a small part of my final decision. The helpful suggestions and the personal

BRIDE BEWARE

If a bridal salon tells you that it has the exclusive on a certain designer's line, you can check this by calling the manufacturer directly to verify that the store is an authorized dealer. It could be trying to pass off "look-alike" gowns that are made by "replica" manufacturers.

attention is what separated great service from mere selling. Stop, take time, and consider all of these things before you make any deposits.

Most brides agree that qualified sales personnel who are experienced and show their sensitivity to a bride's needs are usually found at the most respected and successful salons.

Mary Jo, of Boulder, reminds brides to include important wedding traditions.

My mother bought my "new" gown for me. My mother-in-law "borrowed" me the string of pearls that she wore on her wedding day. My grandmother gave me the crocheted linen handkerchief that had been stored in her lingerie drawer for years. The garter I wore was a shower gift and was baby blue in color.

Although there are no set rules about who provides these lovely "traditional" accessories, it is usually the immediate family or the maid of honor who makes sure that something old, something new, something borrowed, and something blue are a part of the bride's wedding day attire.

Monica, of Little Rock, lists her ten commandments of bridal gown buying.

I am one of six sisters. As an experienced group, we would like to let brides everywhere know our "how-to successfully buy a bridal gown" plan.

1. While it is wise to shop around, visit no more than four shops in one day.
2. Try on various styles, but no more than six at any one shop.
3. Take only one person (your mom or maid of honor) with you to give you an interested yet honest opinion.
4. Have your shopping companion keep notes about the gowns you like best at each location.
5. After all of the looking is completed, sit down together, over a cup of coffee, and narrow the choices to the top three.

6. Revisit just those shops and work with the same salesperson.

7. Try on various headpieces and veils with those select gowns.

8. Ask who the manufacturer is. If the store refuses to tell you, go to another store. You can call the manufacturer directly to see if that shop is an authorized dealer, or if it is trying to pass a "look-alike" off as a designer original.

9. Call the Better Business Bureau to find out if the stores with your "best" choices are on record for any unresolved consumer complaints.

10. Choose "the" dress and put your one-third deposit down knowing your decision has been fully researched.

Special bridal gown "sales" have brought mixed reviews. These experiences will help you to understand what these "sales" really mean.

Nikki, of New Haven, was thrilled with her "sample" wedding gown.

I did not order my wedding dress. Instead, I went to an advertised "sample sale" at one of the full-service bridal salons in my city. These "samples" are gowns that brides tried on before they ordered their own custom gowns and now had been discontinued by the manufacturer. I found a gorgeous beaded gown that was altered to "custom fit" me. I was able to pick up my beautifully pressed gown two weeks after I purchased it and even with the alteration charges, I still saved 40 percent off the ticket price. I strongly recommend this to other brides.

Terri, of Greeley, Colorado, warns about the bridal bargain at traveling bridal shows.

When a giant sale was advertised at a local hotel, I was intrigued by their ad for designer gowns at 80 percent off the regular price. The sale was sponsored by a national distributor and was in our city for one day only. The ballroom at the hotel was divided into rows by portable racks filled with gowns marked with big signs indicating the price ranges. Makeshift dressing rooms did allow me to try on the dresses. All sales were cash and carry. I found a beautiful dress at a marked savings. It appeared that the alterations I needed, and would have to have done elsewhere, would be simple. Well, the sale sponsor was long gone and I had no recourse when I discovered, after talking to several tailors, that the hand-beaded lace trim around the hemline was going to cost a small fortune to remove, cut, and reattach for my height. I didn't really save much after all.

Nora, of Valdosta, Georgia, urges brides to watch out for "bridal brokers."

I had never heard of a "bridal broker," but my friend called my attention to a small ad in our local newspaper bridal section. This "broker" worked out of her home, thereby cutting out expensive overhead, she said, in order to pass savings along to me. She told me to bring in my favorite gown pictures from pages of bridal magazines and she could order directly from the manufacturer, thus cutting out the middleman. She bragged about being able to order from over 100 different manufacturers. To get this 40 percent discount, I had to pay in full for the dress when I ordered it. All sales were final. I also had to pay for the shipping, freight, and insurance on my order. My sales slip clearly stated that I was fully responsible for the size I was ordering, as well as any color variations. I was told that the gown would be shipped directly to my home. Later, much later (15 to 20 weeks later), I was told that the delivery time was longer because indirect routes were used. Yes, she had access to 100 different manufacturers that were actually third-party companies that made "replica" gowns. Incorrect or damaged merchandise was a chance I was taking. My contract said I had five days from receipt of merchandise to make any claims. Her only means of making restitution to me when I received the gown with the hemline ruffle sewn on the sleeve was to give me the name of a seamstress who could fix it—at my own expense.

Fact: *Most full service bridal salons stock on average 15 bridal lines.*
Fact: *Bridal stores can order any gown from any of the bridal magazines.*
Fact: *Fewer than 50 quality bridal manufacturers exist in the world.*

Renting bridal wear is another option available throughout the United States, but from my own experience, most brides want that special gown to be their very own. They know full well that they will only wear it once, yet this dress is very "special." Like their husband, they want it for keeps.

Faye, of Muncie, Indiana, chose another option—she sewed her own gown.

I sew a lot of my own clothes and when I became engaged, I wanted to sew my own custom-made gown. Thank goodness I had my talented mother to help me—it is true when they say that you can be too close to something. With the contemporary patterns and fabulous fabric selections available, I was able to create a $1,000 "look-alike" for about $300. Besides, I'm saving it for my daughter to wear.

Gail, of Shreveport, Louisiana, wore an heirloom wedding gown.

I wanted my wedding to be filled with nostalgia. So, wearing my mother's vintage gown was the greatest idea I had ever heard of. It cost me $200 to have the sleeves altered and to have it professionally cleaned and pressed. At the reception, we even displayed photographs of both of our parents on their wedding days. No one was prouder than I to carry on a family tradition, except maybe my mom, who smiled while tears of pride rolled down her cheeks.

April, of Ashland, Kentucky, relates her father's funniest line about her wedding gown.

My bridal gown was so expensive that my father muttered, "She just drove my car up the aisle."

Have you considered reusing your wedding gown? Here are two stories with two very different opinions.

WEDDING LORE

Most people associate a white dress with purity. Actually, white, according to the ancient Greeks, was the supreme symbol of joy—most appropriate for a wedding.

Carolyn, of Washington, D.C., explains how she was able to wear her wedding gown twice.

Recycling is an important issue in the '90s. I feel that I have helped by wearing my wedding gown twice. The first time was on my wedding day, and the second was to a dance held in our honor, the weekend after our honeymoon. The dance was held by my parents in my hometown, and most of my friends, who could not attend my out-of-town wedding, had not seen it.

Vanessa, of Detroit, regrets that she was a friend in a time of need.

I am sharing my disappointment so that other women will be spared. I was married two years ago in a picture-perfect church wedding. All who attended said it was the most beautiful wedding they had ever seen. I wore a designer's wedding gown that cost $2,400. It was satin and beautifully beaded. When a very close friend of mine announced her engagement, she asked if she could wear my wedding gown, and I said yes. I have never regretted a decision more than that one. I gave it to her in perfect condition— and it was returned to me in such a sorry state, I cried. She had perspired profusely, and someone spilled red wine on it. Although the garment was sent to the best dry cleaner in town, it was totally ruined. The wine stains were not visible, but that area was visibly damaged. Some beads had apparently come off in the cleaning— and were replaced with beads of poorer quality, and not the right size. I am crying as I write this but I want to emphasize to brides— if you value your wedding dress, don't let anyone else wear it. I was unselfish, and now I'm sorry.

Cheryl, of Trenton, New Jersey, tells about her "11th-hour" wedding gown.

My beautiful wedding gown was stolen from my hotel room the night before my wedding. My bridal consultant saved the day, however, by calling the department store, paging the buyer at an afternoon football game, and escorting him back to the store where another gown was substituted. Two seamstresses literally finished sewing the hem just as the wedding march started.

Denise, of Meridian, Mississippi, has some good news for large-size brides.

Since high school I have worn a size-16 dress. When I became engaged, I was frightened to death about going to a bridal shop to try to fit into or possibly rip a gown. Was I surprised when I discovered that big beautiful brides are in and that bridal salons now carry several larger-size styles in stock that you can actually try on. At last bridal manufacturers realize that there are other sizes besides "10."

Statistics tell us that 40 percent of the women in the United States wear size 14 or larger. Heightened interest in athletics, a less nutritious diet, and larger bone structures in women today are the reasons manufacturers cite for their addition of "plus size" bridal styles that offer figure-flattering selections.

Deborah, of Salem, Oregon, tells how the reference to bridesmaids as "ladies in waiting" really fits her experience.

My attendants, all seven of them, were waiting and waiting and waiting for dresses that never arrived. My grandmother thought of a solution. We searched through everyone's closets and voilà! I had a rainbow of pastel prom dresses for my wedding.

Lori, of Green Bay, Wisconsin, explains that if you are searching for bridal bargains, you might consider her mother's money-saving idea.

In these recessionary times, my cost-conscious mother got a brilliant idea. Instead of buying my bridesmaid dresses at a bridal salon, we purchased them "off the rack" of a local department store. Through the four store locations in our city, we were able to find moderately priced floral dresses in all the sizes we needed. In the same way, our groomsmen bought the same dark suits and all wore solid-color ties that matched the color of the bridesmaid dresses. The wedding was beautiful, and my attendants could not have been happier.

Lucky is the bride who marries in old shoes.
—Anonymous

Carla, of Cheyenne, Wyoming, warns that there are blue dresses and there are blue dresses—watch those dye lots!

I just loved royal blue as a color for bridesmaids. I had five girls in my wedding party, and two of them were away at school when I ordered the dresses for the other three maids. During their school break, my two other friends and I went back to the bridal shop and they tried on and ordered their dresses. The first three gowns came in and we were delighted. The color and style looked great on all of the girls. Then came the shock. The second shipment arrived and the two other dresses were a totally different "shade" of blue. The bridal salon was very efficient and was able to return all five dresses, which were exchanged for five of the exact same color. But the waiting and worrying about how they would look was nerve wracking. Brides can save time and trouble from the lesson I had to learn the hard way.

The same rule applies to shoes. It is wise to have all the maids purchase their shoes at the same store. If they are fabric shoes, all the pairs should be brought in at the same time to be dyed together—making sure the color will be consistent. Another big word of caution—don't have the shoes and/or matching handbags dyed in the week prior to the wedding. The dye needs a good amount of time to dry completely. Otherwise, your maids could have colored hands and feet on the wedding day.

Sara, of Fitzgerald, Georgia, has a wonderful idea for the future use of bridesmaid dresses.

My matron of honor was very practical. She arranged to have a local resale shop buy the entire lot of bridesmaid gowns that were worn at my wedding. All of the bridesmaids were delighted to know that they were each guaranteed a "rebate" on their expenditure.

For those dresses that have a definite "bridesmaid look," women can also consider having an evening skirt made from the bottom half of the dress, or they can also recoup some of the expense by selling them to a local theater group or a high school or college drama department.

The biggest concern of the mothers of the bridal couple is what will they wear. Here's how Barbara, of Miami, pleased everyone.

Although I have read that the mother of the bride selects her outfit first and then describes it to the mother of the groom, we used a more contemporary approach. We showed the mothers the picture of my gown and the bridesmaid dresses. We talked about our wedding style together. Each mother selected "her color" and was then able to go shopping with confidence.

Louise, the mother of a bride from Lake Charles, Louisiana, asks, "How does your bridal seamstress measure up?"

I am a special mother of a bride because I am also a bridal seamstress. Everyone complains about alterations and how shops make "extra" money on this service. What they don't know is that, like most of the craftsmen in this field, I have spent 20 years "custom-fitting" brides. In addition to my measuring tape, I use the manufacturer's size chart and suggest the size closest to the bride's largest measurements. Alterations can mean "take in" or "let out," but in either case, it is unnecessary to order a gown two sizes larger, and usually two fittings are all that are needed. At the first fitting, I pin the dress to make all necessary adjustments, and I also bustle the train. At the final fitting, I check the fit and make any added alterations if needed. My fingers work quickly, but I take great pride in my quality.

I am sure that every bride reading this book wishes she could hire you.

Hot bridal accessories for the '90s include bold beautiful jewelry to show off bare necklines and portrait collars. Sophisticated, simple fluid fabrics with sculpted details, ribbon, and metallic trims highlight today's detachable wedding veils. Beaded handbags and decorative "real" flower shoe clips finish the bride from head to toe.

Shelly, of Somerville, Massachusetts, has some advice about ordering tuxedos.

We ordered five tuxedos for our groomsmen and my fiancé got his tux free. The tuxedo shop also honored a coupon that I had gotten at a local bridal show which was good for an additional 10 percent discount on the total order. We placed our initial order in October for our December wedding. At that time, we were told that our groomsmen would have to come into the shop for their individual measurements by no later than one week before the wedding day. Our tuxedo service was just great and the savings were even greater.

Two months prior to the wedding is ideal for the initial ordering of your wedding tuxedos. However, for the months from prom time in April through the popular summer wedding months, it is wise to place your order three months in advance.

What accessories should a fashionable groom of the '90s be looking for? White pleated wing-tip shirts finished with classic bow ties and cummerbunds or vests. Matching fabrics in plaids, paisleys, metallic fabrics, and moirés. Color can also coordinate with the bridesmaids' dress color. Some grooms are now choosing colorful, witty suspenders. Many people do not know that everything comes with a tuxedo rental, including shirt studs and cuff links. Even matching shoes can be rented.

∽

Your bridal attire is the "regal costume" that you wear at your very own royal pageant. Shop, try it on, experiment with colors, and consult with bridal fashion experts. Take your time and select the gown that makes you feel "like a queen."

BRIDAL BARGAIN

If your groom will be attending corporate parties and annual conventions for his job, it may be wise for him to buy his tuxedo.

CHAPTER 9

Guests and Invitations

GUEST AND INVITATION FACTS TO KNOW

---

1. Compile the Guest List Shortly After the Wedding Date Is Announced.
2. A Card-File System Is the Easiest Way to Organize the List and Avoid Duplication.
3. Any Person Invited to Your Wedding Ceremony Should Also Be Invited to Your Reception Party.
4. Invitations Range in Price from $25 to $625 per 100. Decide What Your Invitation Budget Will Be and Expect to Deposit 50 Percent When You Place the Order.
5. Invitations Should Be Mailed Six to Eight Weeks Before the Wedding Date.
6. Wedding Announcements Should Not Be Mailed Until the Day *After* the Wedding.

The Wedding Guests

After the engagement is announced, the first task to be performed by both families is the writing of the guest lists. The problems involved in organizing this task are featured here. They include whom to invite, lists that are too large, out-of-town guests, and unusual circumstances. Today, ordering invitations is less of a problem than how to word them. The stories below discuss proper protocol, and provide the answers to everything you always wanted to ask about guest etiquette.

Ellen, of Berwick, Louisiana, wondered how to determine the correct number of guests for a wedding.

When I became engaged and we announced the news to our parents, we didn't know how to decide fairly about the number of guests to invite. A co-worker who was recently married told me the general rule they followed. The party who is hosting the event determines what number times approximately $25 (the average per person cost of food and refreshments for a four-hour celebration) they can afford. That total is then divided into three parts: the bride's family, the groom's family, and the bridal couple's friends.

It is also important to know that statistically, about one-fourth of the total number invited will not attend.

Kathy, of Rochester, New York, tells about her industrious mother-in-law.

My mother-in-law really surprised and endeared herself to me by handing me her completed guest list the evening I mentioned that we should begin putting a list together. When I began to list all the people I wanted to invite to my wedding, I made up a form that I duplicated for both sets of parents. The paper was 8-1/2 by 11 inches and was divided into eight sections. Each section had space for the complete name, address, city, state, zip code, and telephone number. The bottom line contained the number of children, their names and ages. On the top of each form, I had typed the words FAMILY-FRIENDS-BUSINESS ACQUAIN-TANCES. As the families completed these forms, it was easy to circle the category and to separate the "must be invited" from the "shall we include them?" sheets. I then proceeded to cut the sheets into eight cards, which I used for addressing the invitations. It really was an easy way to keep the who's who organized.

The telephone number is especially important because invitations can get lost in the mail. It is not only proper, it is wise to call back anyone who has not responded by two weeks before the wedding.

Melissa, of Lansing, Michigan, did not know how to handle this kind of situation.

I received replies to my wedding invitations considerably after the date given on the response card. I assumed that because people did not reply, they would not be attending. So, I proceeded to invite others and simply told those who replied so late that the invitation was no longer valid because the food order had had to be verified.

For an event as expensive and elaborate as a wedding can be, perhaps guests today need to be told that proper etiquette requires that they respond immediately, and certainly not later than the date requested. However, it is also proper and wise that the bride of the '90s check back about unanswered invitations before she does a second mailing. A wedding invitation does not have an expiration date.

Angela, of Campbell, California, put it in plain simple language.

R.S.V.P. are the abbreviations for four French words that, in English, mean, please reply. With all of the confusion about the return of response cards and the importance of them, how

---

BRIDAL BARGAIN

Thermography has replaced expensive engraved invitations. This new process produces raised, shiny lettering that literally looks identical to the other and costs less than one-half the price.

else are we supposed to know how much food to prepare? We solved this problem before it happened by inserting a response card in the invitations that was printed with instructions. It said "Please return this card with a *Yes, we will attend* or *No, we will not attend. A stamped envelope is enclosed for your convenience.*" It worked! We didn't have to call a single person on our guest list.

Brides would be wise to heed this cost-effective concept.

Karen, of Auburn, Washington, has some ideas for what to do when the numbers get out of control.

After compiling all the names from both sides of our families, we discovered that we were way over our budgetary limit. To solve this, we simply invited the children of only our immediate families to our wedding celebration.

Cynthia, of Pasadena, has another suggestion.

We had a small wedding to which only our immediate families were invited. We sent a Reception Only invitation to all of our friends and business associates.

If you have too many names, the order of elimination is: (1) guests of unmarried friends; (2) business associates; (3) parents of attendants; (4) people who live more than two hours away; and (5) second cousins.

To invite the children or not to invite the children? These stories address the question.

Lori, of St. Cloud, Minnesota, excluded all children.

My fiancé and I were married in a very formal evening wedding with a reception party following. We did not invite any children simply by not including their names on any invitations and by having our families follow up by passing the word around.

The only children that have to be invited to a wedding are the brothers and sisters of the bridal couple.

Trish, of Roanoke, Virginia, has a great idea for families with many children.

Our family has a lot of school-age children, including babies and toddlers. To avoid a noisy, disturbing ceremony, we sent

---

Wedding Lore

A large wedding in the '90s can be a 12-hour celebration beginning with a morning ceremony and concluding with a full evening reception including dancing. The national average attendance is 300 guests. In the mid-16th century, however, weddings were "festivals" that featured beef, bread, ale, and dancing that continued for ten days and entertained thousands of townspeople as the guests.

separate invitations to those people and their children for the reception only. The reaction was surprising. They liked the idea of not having to run back and forth with the children and enjoyed having plenty of time throughout the day to get everyone ready for the "party" that they were really looking forward to attending.

The invitation clearly gives the guests a written notice of whose presence is requested. If a name is not included on the inner envelope, it is intentional. With the average wedding reception now totaling over $19,000, there has to be a limit.

Laura, of Titusville, Florida, gives some helpful advice about group invitations.

I work in an insurance office. There are 12 young women like myself who sit in one large room at their work centers. Although I am close to all of them, I did not feel obligated to allow them to bring dates to my wedding. In a case where I knew that my co-worker was long-term dating or engaged to someone, I wrote both her name and her companion's full name on the inner envelope of my wedding invitations. For the rest, I wrote only the name of my co-worker on the envelope.

This bride's invitation etiquette was perfect. It is never appropriate to write "and Guest." Rather, it is up to the bride or her family to get the name of the companion or fiancé and send the invitation including that name. And for the single women, a wedding is a perfect and romantic place to meet members of the opposite sex.

Janet, of Hollywood, cautions about "posting" an invitation.

I would never post an invitation on the bulletin board at work again. We had formally invited 125 and 300 showed up.

Susanne, of Bishop, Texas, suggests a way to handle co-workers.

I was a college instructor and worked with every student in the school (about 800). They knew my fiancé as well. Some of my co-workers were close friends, so we invited them to both our ceremony and reception. The rest were all notified (on the bulletin board) with a wedding announcement.

Best advice about inviting guests: Never send an invitation to people you hope won't come—they always do.

Dianna, of Leland, North Carolina, asks, "Have you considered using wedding announcements?"

My family and I decided to have a small wedding with our immediate family only. To share our happy news with everyone else, we sent out wedding announcements. It provided a formal yet cost-effective way to make our marriage officially known.

Announcements are sent out immediately after the wedding day. They are usually sent to friends, business associates, and long-distance relatives. Wedding announcements, by the way, carry absolutely no obligation for a gift.

Marcia, a relative of a bride in Washington, D.C., ponders the "wedding gift" question.

My cousin, who was a bridesmaid in my wedding party, was married in a private ceremony in Hawaii. I did not attend but did receive an announcement. We had been close as children, and I wanted to acknowledge her marriage, so I felt I should send her a wedding gift.

This is entirely your decision. Whether it is an expensive keepsake or a beautiful card, you are sending it because you want to, not because you have to. The receipt of a wedding invitation does not require the guest automatically to send the bridal couple a gift.

Irene, a relative of a bride in Duluth, Georgia, discusses a '90s wedding query.

My niece recently sent us an invitation to the commitment ceremony for herself and her female lover. They have lived together and now were throwing a big bash with vows and a full reception party. We do not approve of her lifestyle, and we would have been very uncomfortable attending. We lied about a previous planned trip and did not attend.

Your niece's invitation was merely an inquiry about attending. It was not a referendum asking for your opinion. Neither was an excuse, made up or otherwise, necessary. However, it is appropriate to send a congratulatory wish for their happiness, despite how you might feel about how that happiness is achieved.

What about out-of-town guests? All special friends and relatives should be invited to your wedding, no matter how far away they may live.

Suellen, of Miami, offers some unique travel advice.

I invited my long-distance relatives to my wedding last August. I even sent copies of the latest AAA travel route (I am a club member) for those who were going to be driving.

Dora, of San Jose, advises brides to use free hotel references.

I sent invitations to my retired aunts and uncles. I mailed them out eight weeks in advance instead of the usual six so that they had plenty of notice. After I received their acceptances, I immediately sent brochures, gladly supplied by the hotel where the reception was going to be held, so that they could make their reservations.

You may also consider car rental brochures as well as brochures from museums, stores, unique restaurants, or any other places of interest to visit while they are in for your wedding.

Luann, of Lake Forest, Illinois, describes her "weekend" wedding.

Because our family is scattered across the United States, my wedding was a love celebration and a family reunion in one. We planned a full weekend of activities that included an informal barbecue, the rehearsal dinner party, and a family-style brunch the day after the wedding. The itinerary was listed on a separate printed card that was included with their invitations.

Another great way to allow his family and your family to mingle and get to know each other is to seat them next to each other, thereby encouraging new friendships and introducing single guests.

Some brides welcome their out-of-town guests by having surprises waiting for them in their hotel rooms. Ideas include:

- basket of fresh fruit and snacks
- bottle of champagne
- box of scented soaps
- box of quality chocolates
- basket of hometown specialties
- the city's local magazine

Most important, each bride stresses the necessity of an attached note that expresses how happy she is that her guests have been able to come.

The Invitations

From elegantly engraved to color-copied postcards, invitations come in every size, color, and paper texture. Some arrive in moiré envelopes, some play music, and some even come gift-wrapped in boxes. Any color ink is acceptable. As a matter of fact, the wedding of the '90s is totally color coordinated. Napkins, centerpieces, floral decorations, even the table covers and napkins match or complement the wedding color scheme.

Lois, a relative of a bride in New Orleans, suggests the use of a calligrapher's services to give your invitation a very formal, elegant look.

I was a bridesmaid at my cousin's wedding. I am a calligrapher and as my wedding gift, I offered to address her invitation envelopes for 400 guests.

Undoubtedly your cousin was grateful to be the recipient of the talent and attention that your generous wedding gift supplied. The typeface, which is the style of lettering you use for the invitations, is purely a matter of personal taste. At least 20 styles are fitting for a traditional wedding proclamation.

Lynn, of Richmond, California, describes a '90s alternative to calligraphy.

Have you ever heard of computerized calligraphy? It provides instant fancy type that is less than half the cost of hand-lettered art. The many styles available will give an impressive and professional look but will not provide the personalized flourishes and unique effects that only an individual's hand can create.

Carrie, of Vancouver, Washington, offers some helpful tips about ordering and mailing your invitations.

Order plenty of extra invitations and envelopes—at least two dozen. You'll need them for additions and mistakes.

Annette, of Pittsburgh, suggests starting ahead—to save time.

Many brides may not know that you can get the envelopes for your invitations ahead of time. In that way, you will be able to have them all addressed and ready for assembly and mailing when your printed inserts are finished.

It is also important to know that with mail being processed today by machines, the zip code should be at least half an inch from the bottom and one inch from the right-hand edge of the envelope. Post offices everywhere have national zip code directories that are free to use at the post office. You can also purchase a small version of your own at local bookstores.

Wedding invitations are becoming physically larger and more elaborate than ever. Some even play the wedding march when opened. It is wise to take a completed, assembled sample to your post office to verify the weight and, most important, the cost of mailing.

Ellen, of Riverside, California, offers some unique invitation ideas.

I consider myself to be a very contemporary woman, and I wanted my wedding invitations to be "different." So I chose to have a telegram delivered to each of the 50 guests I invited.

BRIDE BEWARE

If you are planning to have a professional calligrapher hand-letter your invitation envelopes, expect to pay at least $3 per set (inner and outer envelopes). Costs will vary depending on lettering style, number of lines per envelope, and when the finished pieces must be ready.

Jean, of Lake Tahoe, Nevada, suggests an even bigger surprise.

Balloons and balloon decorations are a very popular and inexpensive way to provide lavish decorations. I took the idea one step further by having my invitations printed on a 12-inch balloon. We mailed the flat balloon inside a greeting card that had a metallic cover with the word "celebrate" imprinted on it. When the guests opened the card, they had to blow up the balloon to read the invitation. My family and friends thought it was one of the cleverest ideas they had ever seen.

Melissa, of Palm Beach, wanted to be different.

I sent postcards that featured a composite of my husband's and my baby pictures. At the bottom of the picture was printed "You've heard of prearranged marriages." On the back side: "We've always been meant for each other! Join us in our celebration of love."

These creative fun invitations are great. They are, however, more appropriate for informal weddings. Most couples still opt for the more sophisticated invitation for their formal wedding.

Judy, of Newbury Park, California, showed great creativity with this idea.

I work at a greeting card store at our local mall. There I discovered an inexpensive item that gave my invitations a very formal look. It's an embosser that can include up to five lines of type. I embossed my return address on the back flap of my invitation envelope. Another plus is that because my husband and I are now living at this same address, I also used it for Christmas cards and my first formal dinner party.

Sherrie, of Minneapolis, suggests some great keepsake ideas.

One of my bridesmaids gave me a beautiful hand-crafted wedding gift. She began with my wedding invitation. She added some flowers and ribbon trim that matched my wedding color scheme. She even added two miniature champagne glasses and framed all of this in a wooden shadow box that she also painted in my wedding color. I will cherish it always.

A great way to remember who attended your wedding is to appoint a special person to stand at the end of your receiving line so that guests can "sign" in your special guest book as they enter.

Sandy, of Louisville, Kentucky, suggests a memento with a purpose.

Before I mailed my wedding invitations, I sent both mothers several unsealed sets to keep as wedding mementos. I also included a note telling them when the invitations were going to be mailed out, so that they would be ready for the phones to start ringing.

Wedding programs are also a great keepsake for all of your guests. Additionally, they can serve as a courteous convenience by having a map to the reception hall on the back side.

Most important of all—don't forget to send an invitation to yourself. Have a family or bridal party member bring one to the post office the day of your wedding. Not only will you have a special keepsake, it will be postmarked with your wedding date and city!

CHAPTER 10

Cake and Flowers

CAKE FACTS TO KNOW

1. The Wedding Cake Is the Official Food of a Wedding Reception Party.
2. The Cake Can Be Any Shape or Size.
3. The Cake's Ornamentation Can Be as Unusual or Elaborate as You Desire.
4. The Top Layer of the Wedding Cake Is Traditionally Saved and Eaten on Your First Anniversary.
5. A Baker Should Welcome You to "Taste Test" the Goods at the Bakery.
6. Cake Flavors and Fillings Should Be Your Favorites. (Banana, Cheesecake, Raspberry, Carrot—Choose Whatever You Like.)

FLOWER FACTS TO KNOW

1. Contact the Florist Four to Six Months Before the Wedding.
2. A Bridal Bouquet May Be Any Color.
3. Attendants' Flowers Should Harmonize with Their Dresses.
4. The Groom's Boutonniere Should Be Different from the Groomsmen's.
5. The Delivery Time and Reception Floral Setup Should Be Discussed.
6. Ask About Wedding Flower Bouquet Preservation.

The Wedding Cake

How do brides select their bakers? What difficulties do they encounter with the ordering and delivery of the cake? Here are the details about this significant wedding food.

Holly, of Cincinnati, offers ideas for clever cake decorations.

Our baker told us of several unique ideas for our wedding cake. He suggested that the wedding cake could be the centerpiece of our bridal table—thus eliminating the need for an additional and costly floral centerpiece. He also suggested a separate small round table on which the cake could be placed and decorated with fresh flowers and surrounded by the bridesmaids' bouquets as a decorative touch.

Many bridal couples want to save the top layer of their cakes for their first anniversary celebration. New ideas have surfaced across the country with regard to this tradition.

Elizabeth, of Salinas, California, tells about a special "Anniversary Cake."

We wanted to have the top layer of our wedding cake put away until our first anniversary. Our baker had two good ideas. He told us to buy a special freezer-proof container in which to store the cake, since just storing it in its cardboard box will give the cake a stale, old taste after that long of a time. He also came up with a new, better idea. If we chose to, he would supply us with a free gift certificate which entitled us to a freshly baked tiny cake decorated in our wedding colors, redeemable for our first anniversary. That way, he said, it avoided the possibility of staleness, and we could enhance wedding tradition by cutting our first slices of cake from the top layer of our wedding cake.

Both of these ideas are practical. In addition, the top tier of the wedding cake could be a "fruit cake" (the traditional groom's cake). This type of cake will store well. It can also be cut into small pieces and given to your guests to take home. (Tradition has it that unmarried women who sleep with that piece of wedding cake under their pillow will dream of the man they will marry.)

Leslie, of Cathedral City, California, asks if you ever heard of the original French wedding cake.

As far back as the 16th century, the classic French wedding cake has been a pyramid of tiny creme-filled puffs of pastry stacked to a peak. Over the puffs is poured a rich caramel sauce. This wedding cake is also different because there is no cutting necessary. Each guest simply helps himself or herself to a puff or two.

Ways to save cake costs:
- Give the appearance of a large expensive cake, but don't tell anyone that the bottom half is really a Styrofoam dummy cake.
- Use "home bakers," who work out of their own kitchens and add their personal home-baked flavor and freshness to your masterpiece.

Suzanne, of Chicago, describes her unique "wedding bell cake."

I wanted a wedding cake to really remember. I am an art teacher so my imagination went wild with ideas. I found an "at-home" baker who was known for her excellent cakes and who was also willing to work with me. My wedding cake was shaped like a huge wedding bell. The baker's husband even built an arch and a swinging pendulum with a flat platform on which the cake was constructed. It actually swung back and forth!

Other brides who like unusual looks in wedding cakes should ask their bakers about art deco decorated cakes or rolled fondant (that is a smooth marzipan frosting that became popular during the Victorian era).

WEDDING LORE

At their 1981 wedding, Lady Diana and Prince Charles had a 255-pound, hexagonal, rum-flavored, traditional English fruit cake, which took 11 weeks to create.

Here is a 1990s version of a century-old tradition. Kay, of Virginia Beach, describes her European sweet table.

For our wedding, our caterer prepared a Viennese table that featured an assortment of pastries, cookies, finger foods, miniature fruit tarts, and eclairs to which guests could help themselves.

Kathy, of Fort Lauderdale, suggests another clever cake concept.

My wedding cake was a series of five layers, one smaller than the other, on which chocolate-dipped fruits, truffles, and petit fours were beautifully arranged. Everyone remarked about the uniqueness of this idea.

Just as the flavors of wedding cake fillings and frostings have become elaborate, so too have the costs. Expect to pay between $1.00 and $4.00 per serving for your wedding cake. The general guideline is that no more than 3 percent of your total wedding budget should be spent on this nuptial finery. Many bakers can suggest ideas for types of cakes to help you save money. Some include the delivery charge right in the base cake price, and some even supply a special cake knife as part of their package.

Barbara, of Mount Prospect, Illinois, wondered if a wedding cake could be served as "dessert."

Our baker suggested that our wedding cake be our dessert. We thought it might look "cheap," but after talking to other couples who had recently married and did this, we felt comfortable "officially" cutting the cake immediately after we finished eating, and then having the banquet servers cut and serve the cake to everyone.

It is considered an honor to cut your wedding cake and serve it to your guests. Today many couples also include a groom's cake. The bride's cake is usually served as dessert, while the groom's cake is cut and boxed for guests to take home as a wedding treat.

Karen, of Milton, Vermont, explains the "groom's cake" concept.

The groom's cake usually reflects his hobbies or interests, such as a cake shaped like a computer, a fish, a golf ball, or a top hat. A friend of mine even passed out chocolate cigars in lieu of a traditional groom's cake. The origin of the groom's cake dates back to ancient Israel, when people journeyed great distances for weddings. These cakes, baked by the groom's parents, were for the guests' trip home.

Renee, of Columbus, Ohio, tells how wedding bells and lovebirds are now being replaced by special porcelain keepsake cake tops.

For my wedding shower, I received a delightful cake topper from my maid of honor. It was made by Precious Moments. It had an angelic couple dressed in wedding attire made completely of porcelain. Not only was it prominently placed on top of our cake, it now sits proudly on a special shelf next to our wedding portrait. We plan to continue collecting these darling figurines for other important events in our married life.

Special ornaments like this are also available from other companies that advertise in bridal magazines. Bridal couples can even request replicas of themselves, including the color of the tuxedo, their hair color, even a mustache or beard for the groom if he sports one.

Pam, of Cumming, Georgia, sends this valuable message.

Put all details in writing. My baker misunderstood his instructions for my wedding cake. When he checked back with me, just before the wedding day, we discovered that our signals had crossed. He thought I was just changing my mind at the last minute, but I was able to refer back to my written instructions, which clarified the situation and avoided not only hard feelings, but more important, an embarrassing wedding day with *no* wedding cake.

Kelly, of Topeka, Kansas, warns brides to watch the spotlight.

We ordered an outstanding wedding cake to feed 400 people. It included clear plastic pillars and a working water fountain. We ordered this cake three months before the wedding. The cake arrived and was beautifully assembled by the baker. The hall

---

WEDDING LORE

It is an age-old tale that the bride and groom must be the first to cut the cake because if anyone else does, it will cut into their joy and prosperity.
—An old wives' tale

arrived and was beautifully assembled by the baker. The hall manager was so impressed with how it looked that he set up a special spotlight on the cake so everyone was sure to notice and admire it. What we didn't figure on was that the heat from the spotlight would melt the frosting and bend the plastic pillars. By the time we were ready to "cut the cake," the cake looked like a big white-and-pink mud pie. To say the least, in addition to the original $50 setup charge, we paid an additional $50 for the damaged pillars and the clogged fountain that had to be completely cleaned with toothpicks.

If this valuable lesson saves one other couple a casualty like this, it has been more than worth while telling.

Kay, of Rochester, Minnesota, tells about her wedding with no wedding cake.

Our wedding was just wonderful—until it was time for the cutting of the cake. The problem was there was no cake. A catering worker had dropped it earlier, and it literally "exploded." So the caterer substituted a fake wedding cake, made of a hard plasterlike substance. The caterer thought that we could pretend to cut it, for the photos, and the guests would be served other layer cakes that had quickly been brought in. When my husband found out about this, he started arguing with the caterer. Meanwhile, up on the bandstand, the band leader, unaware of what was going on, announced that it was now time for everyone to see us cut the cake. So all the guests turned and looked just in time to see my husband pick up the fake cake, shouting profanities, and throw it right at the caterer.

While this scene created an exciting reception ice breaker, I highly doubt that a "cake throw" could ever become a standard wedding tradition.

Shelly, of Scottsdale, Arizona, describes her unusual wedding cake.

We decided to elope and wanted the romantic setting of a little chapel with a local justice of the peace. We also created our own unique wedding cake. We bought three packages of Hostess cupcakes and some paper plates. We stacked the cupcakes pyramid style on and some paper plates. We stacked the cupcakes pyramid style on the plate, and after the ceremony, we each took a bite of the one on the top of the stack. We proceeded to give one cupcake to the officiant, his wife (who was also the organist), and to our two witnesses. We all laughed as we shared in this memorable meal.

The real wedding cake secret is visual presentation and making certain that this delicious dessert, whatever it may be, is large enough to serve all of your guests.

Flowers

The wedding bouquet is the most important accessory of the bridal ensemble. Whether simple or sensational, flowers have been a bridal necessity since the wedding march began. Here tips on what to know are followed by experiences with flower ordering, costs, silk flowers versus real flowers, and delivery precautions.

Michelle, of Bayshore, New York, describes her florist's special wedding corner.

Our florist had a special bridal corner that she had set up in her shop. Complete with table and chairs and her sample books, she offered cozy, comfortable privacy and even served coffee as she and I leisurely discussed the appropriate floral styles for my wedding.

This warm, caring approach has been the secret of many successful businesses. Flower styles are determined by the formality of the wedding, the budget, and the colors desired.

Tracy, of Griffith, Indiana, offers an important "piece" of advice.

I know florists require that a swatch of the bridesmaids' dress fabric be given to them for flower coordinating, but I'll bet many brides did not know that there are at least seventeen shades of white. To match white roses or other white flowers, it is also a good idea to snip a small piece of the bridal gown inseam for color matching.

Flowers are the most important accessory of your wedding outfit. Kellie, of Plantation, Florida, tells how her bouquet made a fashion statement that was as important as her dress.

I felt like the queen of my own pageant, as I carried an armful of red roses—Miss America style. When the ceremony was over, I added a unique personal touch. After my husband and I left the altar area of the church, I stopped and gave a single rose from my bouquet to both my mother and my new mother-in-law.

Beginning your wedding day with a symbolic gesture of this kind really helps to establish family unity.

Jean, of Clarks Summit, Pennsylvania, reestablished an old-time custom.

My wedding headpiece was quite elaborate. It framed my face and was heavily decorated with beads and pearls. My veil was two-tiered. One shorter veil was used as a "blusher" veil that covered my face as I walked up the aisle, and the longer veil was cathedral length and extended six feet behind me. After the ceremony, I removed the entire headpiece and wore a beautiful wreath made of flowers, beads, and some green leaves. It was certainly more comfortable and allowed me to circulate much more easily.

Before 1850, brides simply wore a flower corsage or a wreath of flower buds. Flowers were also sewn on the wedding veil. After 1850, the formal bridal bouquet was introduced as a bridal accessory.

Tanya, of Cookville, Tennessee, tells about an old-fashioned wedding flower custom that she "reused."

My fiancé and I met at a mutual friend's wedding, where he caught the garter and I caught the bouquet. I have kept this memento in mint condition along with the accompanying garter. We decided that we could perhaps perpetuate a chain, if we too tossed these same lucky wedding souvenirs to another couple.

Flowers that are available year round and are frequently used in bridal bouquets are calla lilies, carnations, gardenias, lilies of the valley, roses, and stephanotis.

Liz, of Sunland, California, offers her "good-luck" flower idea.

Our florist suggested a clever and romantic idea to us. My favorite flower is a gardenia. So she suggested that my wedding bouquet include some or all of that kind of flower. She added that including your favorite flower was also considered a "good-luck" idea. In the same way, one of the flowers used in the bride's bouquet is usually the flower that is featured in the groom's boutonniere. So my husband wore a small gardenia blossom. The fragrance was heavenly, and we are very happy we did this.

Many brides may not know that the stephanotis, a classic wedding flower, is also known as the good-luck flower. The freesia, a close look-alike, is readily available for about half the cost.

Lani, of Phoenix, relays important floral information for all "uniformed" people.

Both my husband and I are police officers. We wanted him and all of our groomsmen (also policemen) to wear their dress uniforms for our wedding. Policy varies across America, but it is necessary to get written permission from the chief of police to accomplish this. A wedding is, in the eyes of the law, an unofficial, unsanctioned event. Permission must also be obtained for boutonnieres as they are not an authorized uniform accessory.

You might also like to know that wedding etiquette dictates that the groom and all of his attendants should be dressed the same—in other words, no usher should be in a tuxedo or a dress suit when all of the others are in uniform.

Sharon, of Houston, tells about her personal crew (her two friends) who decorated her ceremony site with color coordinated balloons instead of flowers.

My personal decorating crew (my two very close friends) created three balloon arches through which my bridal party marched, balloons and wide white ribbon bows to mark the pews, and balloon clusters on the altar. They even gave each guest a balloon on a string, and everyone released them together as the bridal couple left the church. Total items required 200 14-inch colored balloons, a tank of helium (rented), several balls of string, and some very nimble fingers. I will never forget this beautiful colorful gift of love.

The cloth runner usually supplied by the florist for the main bridal aisle at the church or other ceremony site, must be measured individually in order to insure the correct length. Newest trend is the use of 36" wide white lace instead of white cotton fabric.

Jan, of Tampa, Florida, tells what "floral savings" cost her.

Although it is both permissible and cost saving to use floral centerpieces on the altar for your ceremony and then move them to your reception site, I wish I had never done it. We took our formal group wedding photos at the altar after the ceremony. Only after that could the florist rush the flowers over to the reception hall. They arrived seconds before we did, and frankly, it appeared that our guests were wondering where these last-minute table decorations were coming from. I felt very cheap about the way it made our preparations look.

A professional florist is really not *expensive. Here are the three most important facts to note.*

1. You are paying for a professional artist's design sense and skill to create a bouquet to take your breath away.
2. A professional florist knows many tricks about how to create a full and fancy floral effect within a given budget.
3. A professional florist acts as a decorating consultant, ensuring excellent color coordination as well as the correct number of flowers in order to give you the floral fantasy you are dreaming of.

Joyce, a florist in Philadelphia, offers some "inside" floral tips.

Brides complain about the costs of everything including the flowers, yet they wrinkle their noses at the idea of a plastic bouquet

---

BRIDAL BARGAIN

Use potted plants for altar arrangements instead of floral bouquets: gardenias, azaleas, or chrysanthemums are perennials that can be planted later in your own garden.

holder. As an experienced floral designer, I want to tell brides that bouquet holders are available in silver or gold metallic, or they can be sprayed to match any color. Most important, flowers are secured in place with special pins and the Styrofoam core allows water to surround the blossoms all day, thus assuring that they will look fresh and beautiful longer. Hand-tied, hand-wrapped flowers are time-consuming preparations that you, the bride, are paying for.

Brides can also carry one single long-stem rose or several calla lilies in place of a larger more costly bouquet.

Athena, of Brooklyn, tells how to stay within your floral budget.

Be careful of spreading your floral budget too thin. It's better to do one thing well than to do several things halfway. I'm sorry that we used inexpensive altar arrangements for our ceremony just so we could also line the wedding aisle with pew bows. It looked really cluttered and cheap. Rather, concentrate on the altar as the first focal point, since that is where the important pictures of your ceremony are taken. If your budget allows, place decorative bows at alternate pews.

Charise, of Dallas, offers her "fresh" cost-effective idea.

My florist suggested "hairpiece flowers," a unique and new fresh flower idea, instead of fabric bows or hats. It was especially effective for my summer garden wedding. This advice was offered only as another cost-cutting, easy, and pretty idea. My bridesmaids really appreciated the savings.

Carnations are considered the most versatile flower for weddings. They can be tinted any color; they are heat hardy, and they are economically priced.

Jodi, of Scarsdale, New York, tells how "pulling out" saved her wedding day.

My florist suggested a great idea to me. He called it a "pull-out" bouquet. I didn't really want to throw away my wedding bouquet, so in order to throw some of my good luck to the next single woman at the wedding reception, he created a small nosegay within my bouquet, which I simply pulled out after the wedding ceremony and tossed to the single female guests during the traditional bouquet toss.

Another version of this same idea has been used when the bride greets her groom at the altar. There she pulls his boutonniere flower from her bouquet and pins it to his lapel as a symbolic loving gesture.

Garden and party rental companies offer arches, gazebos, candelabras, and champagne fountains for special wedding effects.

Joni, of Marco Island, Florida, explains how silk flowers offer several advantages.

Our florist was just wonderful to work with. Not only did he know of our limited budget, he was able to create for me the exact floral bouquet I had dreamed of carrying—at half the cost. He used silk flowers for the expensive out-of-season orchids I wanted and "look-alike" real flowers for the rest. Silk flowers will never wilt, and they can be tinted and matched to any unusual color tones.

Weddings are expensive celebrations. Traditionally, the bride's family paid for most of the cost. Today, however, marriage is considered a joint expense. One detail in particular that is often misunderstood is that the groom now usually pays for the wedding flowers—all of them.

As in any other business, some florists have been known to deliver poorly constructed bouquets, old flowers, provide generally poor service, or worst of all, be late. Melinda, of Brooklyn, New York, tells this story.

I cried throughout my entire wedding, not because I was overcome by the emotion of the day, but because my wedding flowers arrived at the church as I greeted my fiancé at the altar. There was a huge traffic accident that caused tremendous delays on the freeway—but why me? The florist refunded 50 percent of our money and we were able to take "mock" photos in the church after the ceremony, but the real moment had been totally lost.

BRIDE BEWARE

It is a wise idea to ask all of your bridesmaids if anyone is allergic to any flowers or plants. It would be a shame to have the video of your wedding vows interrupted with sneezes.

A PERFECT TIME FOR
FLOWERS

- *Engagement Night—a mixture of red and white roses symbolizes happy love and unity.*
- *Meeting the Parents— a bouquet of morning glories symbolizes affection.*
- *Engagement Party— red tulips symbolize a declaration of love.*
- *The Bridal Shower— yellow lilies symbolize gaiety.*
- *Bridesmaid Luncheons—small individual bouquets of speedwell express female fidelity.*
- *Bachelor Party—a sprig of ivy stands for fidelity.*
- *Rehearsal Dinner— fresh ivy geraniums are the traditional wedding favor.*
- *Wedding Ceremony— a bouquet of blue violets and lemon blossoms will symbolize your faithfulness.*
- *Family Keepsakes— thank your parents with bell flowers and white periwinkles.*
- *Your Honeymoon— sweet basil or white dittany bring good wishes and passion— have them waiting in your room.*

This experience emphasizes the importance of professionalism and getting the details in writing, including all costs and delivery arrangements. A separate meeting with your florist at the church and reception site will help both of you to understand visually what effect you want to create and what will fit best into your budget. This communication is really necessary to ensure the floral perfection of your wedding day.

Kim, of Boston, offers another floral warning.

Never plan your wedding in the month of February, especially around Valentine's Day. Our flower costs were triple what they would have normally been and the delivery delay was terrible.

The same applies for other holiday times, such as Christmas and Mother's Day.

Susan, of New Orleans, explains how you can be a flower scout.

The way I discovered the "quality" of the florists I was considering was to go to their shop and see how well kept and clean it was. I also made sure to look into their refrigerated cases. If "old" flowers were being stored in there, it was a sure sign to me that "old flowers" would be used as fillers in my bouquets. I quickly eliminated several "recommended" florists who were supposed to have great prices for wedding orders. You cannot really cut corners with so-called bridal bargains. I learned through this scouting process—you get just what you pay for!

The general rule of thumb is that no more than 15 percent of the total wedding budget should be spent on flowers. Today you get what you pay for; if your dream bouquet is a cascade of white orchids, and that is what you really want, be prepared to pay for it.

For any bride who wants to preserve her wedding bouquet, Terry, of Honolulu, tells how to do it the 1990s way!

The microwave oven is one of the best ways to permanently preserve your wedding bouquet. It actually dehydrates the flowers, preserving the colors better than any other method can. Any good microwave cookbook contains easy instructions for how to safely accomplish this "keepsaking process" all by yourself.

For the record, several brides across the country have suggested this cost-effective idea. Be sure to read and follow the directions carefully. *It would be a real shame to zap your wedding bouquet to ashes in one minute or less.*

An experienced florist is also a creative artist. He or she will give you a variety of choices as well as a wide range in price. Usually church floral decorations remain there. Reception flowers, however, can be transported to hospitals, old age homes, or other charities after your event. Extend the floral beauty and happiness of your wedding by sharing them with others.

Music and Entertainment

MUSIC AND ENTERTAINMENT
FACTS TO KNOW

1. Music and Entertainment are *Options* for a Reception Party, Not Requirements.
2. The Average Musical Group Will Perform for Four Hours for a Set Fee.
3. Live Bands Charge an Hourly Overtime Fee.
4. Be Sure to Ask for References.
5. Go to See and Hear, in Person, the Performance of Any Entertainers You Are Considering.
6. Disc Jockey Rates Range from $250 to $500. Live Band Rates Range from $500 to $7,500.
7. It Is Not Necessary to Tip the Entertainers.
8. Put All Arrangements in Writing.

The entertainment provided at the wedding reception is the critical factor in determining the success of the party. A good band, or, more important, a personable band leader, can captivate the crowd and keep everyone interested. Because the entertainment can "make" or "break" the reception, hiring only the best should be a bride's major concern. This chapter lists facts about hiring wedding entertainment and illustrates how to contract with them. Problems related to dealing with bands and DJs as well as entertainment scams are explained. Other traditional customs and unique ideas for ethnic entertainment are also featured.

The ceremony is the most important event of your wedding day. The music that is used should reflect the sacredness of the occasion as well as the love you feel for each other. Cyndie, of Forest Park, Illinois, explains.

Have you ever heard of prelude music? According to our church's musical director, that is music, either instrumental or vocal, that is performed during the 20 minutes prior to the start of the ceremony. For the ceremony itself, he suggested the organ with flute or other string instruments for a unique sound. Trumpets can also enhance the majestic feeling of the procession and recession.

Therese, of Tuscaloosa, Alabama, describes her wedding reception program.

My wedding planner included a chart that detailed the program of my reception party. It included places for the titles of the songs I wanted played at special times, as well as the names of all of the important people involved. I gave this chart to my band leader, who used it as his outline for the evening. It worked perfectly and nothing was overlooked.

This idea is an extension of the ceremony program through which guests can follow along, knowing what songs, singers, musicians, and special speakers will be included in the service.

It's a battle of the bands. Which is better, the live band or the disc jockey? The following stories debate this ultimate question. Jill, of Garland, Texas, explains her choice.

We made up our minds to have live music at our reception after attending another wedding at which a very unfriendly DJ simply announced the evening's events and played randomly selected tapes all evening. Because live band fees are set by the number of musicians included, we decided on a trio of a piano, bass, and drums. The pianist played alone during our cocktail and dinner hour. This worked well because it was strictly background music. The problem started when the music would not carry across our large reception hall filled with 200 guests.

Most experts say there is no such thing as too big a band. A good rule of thumb is one musician for every 25 guests. If you want people to dance, I suggest a minimum of four musicians. And big speakers don't always mean you'll get better sound quality.

Many cities now offer disc jockey referral networks that provide free up-to-date lists of local DJs. This shopping guide offers their names, addresses, and phone numbers. It features a description of their services, including pricing. The bridal couple can deal directly with the individual entertainers. Kay of Lansing, Michigan, did just that.

We decided to use a disc jockey at our wedding reception. Although it was not live music, it offered many advantages. The disc jockey's lively personality enhanced the announcements of our reception activities. He played quality compact discs and was able to read the crowd and easily build the mood by selecting more of the songs the crowd really loved. His space requirements were minimal, yet he used spotlights, a fog machine, and a mirrored ball, which really added fun and unusual excitement to our party.

The bride of the '90s is value driven, particularly when it comes to her wedding entertainment. Thus, the idea of saving up to 50 percent of the cost by using mobile music instead of a live band is certainly something to consider.

Most entertainers require that a deposit of one-third the total cost be paid when you contract with them. The disc jockey, usually a one-man show, costs from $250 to $500. There may also be add-ons for special effects, such as a laser show. On the other hand, the live band's fee is based on the number of musicians in the group, so the costs depend on how many you have.

BRIDE BEWARE

If your reception site has a piano, it may be used for your musical entertainment—if it is tuned. Some hotels may charge you for tuning it. (The average fee is $50.) Otherwise, a band can bring its own piano for an additional fee.

Sue, of San Francisco, warns brides about reception hall "rules" regarding bands.

It is not uncommon for a couple (nor should they feel embarrassed) to stop in at a wedding reception to see the physical appearance of a band, how they sound, and how they work the crowd. But many couples may not realize that they also have to check with their banquet manager about any union rules regarding musical entertainment at their facility. We supplied our band with the name and telephone number of our banquet manager. This put the responsibility for arrangements into the hands of the professionals that we had hired.

Gini, of Rochester, Minnesota, stresses the protection a written contract provides.

My best advice to brides about the music for their receptions is to be specific with your band about the details. Although we agreed about the fee for the band, the element of time was the source of a real argument between us. To begin with, the band (which was supposed to arrive at 7:00) came marching across the room with their equipment as we finished our dessert at 7:45— they had had car trouble. As a result, the setup time took up the first half hour of playing time. They did perform well and took the usual four breaks during the four-hour performance time. However, they stopped playing at 12:00 A.M. We felt that they owed us another half hour, but our contract read 8:00 P.M. to 12:00 A.M. So, the check my father gave them reflected a half-hour deduction. They left angry and have since threatened to sue us. Be careful!

You did the right thing by standing up for your right to four hours of music for a four-hour fee. By admitting that their lateness was their own fault, they really don't have any claim against you.

Emily, of Paramus, New Jersey, found a "happy medium" for her wedding.

We couldn't make up our minds about the kind of music we wanted for our wedding. We wanted a vocalist, but we also wanted to save money. Then we heard about a new kind of service—the sing-along—a professional singer who sings along with tapes. A sing-along entertainer functions both as a DJ and as a singer. We arranged with him the songs we wanted him to sing, and he brought instrumental versions of those songs as well as a mix of regular tapes and CDs. The sing-along entertainment was the best of both worlds. Besides, the sing-along tapes provided the equivalent of a 30-piece band plus a live singer. Our guests loved it, and so did we, especially when he sang our song to us. And the best part about it was that a typical four-hour evening ranges between $400 and $800.

Band networks that operate in a similar fashion to the disc jockey network are also now forming across the country. Their brochures feature a photograph of the band and a full description of its services, including prices. Again, the couple deals directly with the individual entertainers.

Joanne, of Terre Haute, Indiana, offers some timely advice.

My advice to brides is to start looking immediately after you book the reception hall, as popular bands are booked at least a year in advance. More important, if you are planning a holiday wedding, be prepared to pay double the regular fee, especially if your wedding will be on or around New Year's Eve, as ours was. It seems that there is an abundance of work available in many lounges on special days like that, so in order to secure a popular group for your event, you have to make the booking more appealing to them.

Christine, of Raleigh, North Carolina, suggests using a music agency.

Brides should be aware that there are local music agencies that negotiate and book local bands in most cities. They provide one-stop music shopping for bridal couples. Couples come in, relax, and watch videos of several bands that fit the size, style, and cost they are looking for. This service is free to the couple, because the music agent receives his commission from the band. We really liked this because we could see how professional the band looked as well as sounded.

Marlene, of Scarsdale, New York, provides other sources for good bands.

Major cities throughout the U.S. publish a directory of union musicians. Another idea, besides calling banquet managers of local hotels, is to call a recently married couple whose wedding announcement appeared in your local paper.

Carol, of Newport Beach, California, offers some other entertainment options.

Consider having a jazz ensemble or a country/western band with a square dance caller. You can also end the party with a special laser show or a fireworks presentation.

Jill, of Austin, suggests several inexpensive alternatives.

Inquire about using musicians from the music department of your local community college. Or contact private music instructors in your area; if they aren't interested, they can help you to hire their prize pupils. Even friends or relatives may be honored to perform at your wedding.

Ethnic dances can also be featured at your reception party. Whether it's the Irish jig, the Italian Tarantella, or the Israeli hora, a dance can be the highlight of the wedding, as Sara, of Stamford, Connecticut, explains.

We were lifted up on chairs during the hora dance. I was in the air and saw a friend of my new in-laws dancing with my first cousin. Both sides of the family mixed together and danced with us. It was like they were all toasting us.

When the music and the mood is in full swing, everyone wants to dance. European etiquette for dancing requires all groomsmen to dance with many of the women present. (This includes younger women, who would love to be asked.) It is proper for them to dance with each bridesmaid as well as both mothers.

Because 49 percent of all weddings that take place in America now are encore marriages, the big band sound is back. A survey of well-known band leaders provides the following insight.

BRIDAL BARGAIN

Hire a "music buff" friend to organize tape cassettes and play them throughout the reception party.

Music from the '30s and '40s as well as songwriters such as Porter, Gershwin, and Irving Berlin is experiencing a revival. Contemporary classics, '60s dance tunes, and Motown hits are also popular. Traditional dances too, such as the fox trot, the rhumba, and the waltz, are more popular than ever. The most popular requested song for a bride and groom's first dance is "Our Love Is Here to Stay." Other often-requested tunes include: "We've Only Just Begun" and "Daddy's Little Girl."

Christy, of Tacoma, Washington, describes a special father/daughter dance.

At my wedding, my husband and I danced the traditional first dance of the evening to our favorite song. About a month after our marriage, we attended our friend's reception at which a special dance was announced. My friend, the bride, and her father danced all alone to "Daddy's Little Girl." It was such a nice idea, especially because my friend's parents are divorced and my friend is very close to her father.

Denise, of Lincoln, Nebraska, asks if you ever thought about including a grand march at your reception.

Following the first dance, we proceeded with a unique idea to get all of our guests on their feet. We held a grand march that we led, followed by our parents, grandparents, wedding party, and all of the guests. We paraded around the hall, outside and around the building, and back in again. The crowd loved it, and it really set the mood for continued dancing and celebrating.

Mary Ann, of Memphis, explains that performing wedding traditions and customs at your reception also adds to the occasion.

After the guests had arrived and everyone was seated, the best man was the first to participate in the festivities by toasting the new bride and groom. We followed a French custom during which we shared our champagne toast from a two-handled silver goblet shaped like a bowl. In France, a bridal couple proceeds to carry this bowl to each table, and serves each guest a sip to symbolize the sharing of their happiness.

Speaking of toasts, Diane, of Cleveland, tells a story about one you will long remember.

I will never forget our wedding toast—or more to the point, the event that followed it. Our best man made a stunning toast to our future happiness, after which he proceeded to announce that all of the ladies at the reception who still had keys to my husband's apartment should please give them to me, as the groom was no longer available. Fifteen girls sauntered up to the head table and handed me a key. I must admit that it was a well-planned practical joke—and it was quite funny.

Not every bride would find this funny. If you do not like practical jokes, be sure to discuss your feelings with your bridal party. Let them know that you want a dignified affair with no embarrassing surprises.

Nancy, of Westchester, New York, describes a very "different" kind of bouquet toss.

I have many single friends because I was the first of our college sorority group to wed. They all attended my wedding and they all participated in the traditional bouquet toss to see who would be the next to wed. But because I know they are all looking for Mr. Right, I did something different. My florist created a large bouquet of daisies. I stood in the center of the circle of all of my friends. When the moment came, I pulled open the bow tie and one dozen fresh flowers flew through the air in every direction. It was a delightful sight. One daisy had a special yellow bow attached to it, so the woman who caught the flower danced with the man who caught the garter my husband threw.

Charlene, of Austin, suggests her original last-dance-of-the-evening idea.

My husband and I, and our bridal party, came out to the center of the dance floor and formed a circle of love by linking our arms around the people on either side of us. Then we formed an arch with our arms and two by two the guests were invited to join in as they passed under the arch and continued to form a longer arch. After the last couple had passed through, my husband

WEDDING LORE

In Poland, the "dollar dance" was a popular reception activity. By pinning a dollar to the bride's or groom's clothes, men and women bought the right to dance with them at the wedding.

and I passed through the entire bridge of arms and kissed when we reached the end.

Andrea, of St. Paul, Minnesota, describes her grand exit.

As a grand finale to our lively reception, all of the guests gathered on each side of the hotel's exits. Each was given a colored helium balloon, as we exited from the building to our car, and the entire crowd released the balloons into the air as a unique sendoff.

Rose petals, birdseed, and the traditional rice are alternative ways to shower a wedding couple with good wishes as they leave their reception party for their honeymoon.

Holly, of Sacramento, warns that some reception pranks can be carried too far.

It was 4:00 A.M. on my wedding day when my husband's college buddies carried him in. After an hour of bowing to the porcelain chair, he fell asleep. Later, at the reception, his fraternity brothers gave him his traditional paddling, and I spent my honeymoon putting cold packs on his bruised buttocks.

It is not so funny ruining a car with whitewash lettering, or making a bride cry and beg that the groom not be thrown into the swimming pool. Friendly pranks can turn into freakish disasters. Courtesy and caution should be observed for wedding day celebrations.

Your entertainment budget should not exceed 5 percent of your total wedding costs. Music is a universal language that can stir the emotions of even the most serious individual listeners. Great entertainment is the one element of your reception party that your guests will recall with fond memories.

THE BEST THING ABOUT OUR WEDDING WAS:

My parents, bridesmaids, and I decided to walk to the church, in true English tradition. It was a beautiful day, and parading down the street made it feel like my own special pageant.

We had a very special wedding recessional. I have always been described as having a bubbly personality. So, when my husband and I descended from the altar down the aisle, two bubble machines filled the air with delicate shiny bubbles that everyone enjoyed.

We wrote our own vows and I sang a special song to my new husband as part of our ceremony. We put a lot of thought into our feelings for one another and incorporated musical selections that gave our ceremony a special meaning.

The recessional hymn. I'm the youngest child in the family, and my father always joked that when I got married, we should play the *Hallelujah Chorus* by Handel. So, in our wedding program, we wrote "as requested by the bride's father." Everyone laughed when they heard *Hallelujah* ringing throughout the church.

I ordered my bridesmaid dresses from a mail-order catalog. I selected a great style that can be worn again—because I wanted to make it as inexpensive and practical as possible for all my bridesmaids.

The caterer made sure that my husband and I led the buffet line right at the beginning. You always hear how the wedding couple aren't able to eat at their own reception—but we did!

Transportation

An extraordinary day deserves nothing less than extraordinary transportation. Your wedding day is the one day when you want everything to be perfect. "Get me to the church in style" is just as important as "get me there on time." Limousines, fire engines, even helicopters provide transportation options that can give your wedding a special finishing touch. The stories in this chapter feature facts to know about limousine rentals as well as problems that can be connected with limousine services. Special car rentals and unusual get-away vehicles are also discussed.

Alison, of Tucson, Arizona, explains how her wedding began with a flair.

My cousin, a bridesmaid in my wedding party, is very creative. On my wedding day, all the bridesmaids dressed at my home. When we were all ready and walked outside to our cars, there, in my driveway, was a white van all decorated with bells and crepe-paper streamers. On the back was a big beautiful sign that read "The Bridal Van." There was plenty of room for all of us, including my dad and mom, who sat up front, to ride together and really begin the day in a fun and clever way.

This idea is so clever, it could become a national tradition!

Marlene, of New Orleans, suggests that you consider a fleet of limousines for your wedding.

Ours was considered a large wedding. We had six couples and a flower girl in our wedding party. We really wanted to do it up right, so we hired four limousines. Before the ceremony, three limousines came to my house. It was quite a scene as all of the neighbors came out to watch while the three white stretch limos pulled up and parked, in a row, in front of my house. I really felt like "her royal majesty" as I was escorted in the first car with my dad. My mother, my grandmother, and maid of honor rode in the second vehicle, and all the other bridesmaids filled the third car. The fourth limo went to my fiancé's house and transported him and the best man to the church. All of these luxury limos parked and waited in line at the church. Following the ceremony, my husband and I were driven to the reception in limo #1. Both sets of parents rode in limo #2, while the rest of the bridal party were chauffeured to our reception site in limos #3 and #4. People still talk about how grand it was!

BRIDAL BARGAIN

Wedding decorating kits that include bells, streamers, even a JUST MARRIED sign can turn a car into a special wedding vehicle. They are available at stationery stores everywhere.

Brides might also like to know that when ordering a fleet of limousines, you can arrange for a special discount.

Here's important advice from Catherine, of Salem, Massachusetts, for all couples who will have a limousine escorting them on their wedding day.

We were so busy on our wedding day that between the photographer, the reception, and the excitement of going to Hawaii for our honeymoon, we forgot all about our own car. We had used a limousine to transport the wedding party from their homes to the ceremony and to the reception. But nobody thought about driving the groom's car to the reception site so we could get to the airport after the wedding. A quick-thinking hotel manager ordered a cab that got us there just in the nick of time as they were boarding the plane.

Here are two good ways to avoid this problem: Arrange that, on the day before the wedding, the best man drives the groom's car to the reception site; or on the wedding day itself, while the bride and groom are chauffeured by limousine, the best man or another groomsman drives their car from the ceremony to the reception site.

Kelly, of Stamford, Connecticut, reports how limousines truly provide luxury services.

The limousine company we hired was outstanding! They not only brought me to the church and drove us, including our honor attendants, to the hotel where we held our reception, they also took us for a special "short, but sweet" drive along the lake so we could spend a few minutes alone together and have a private champagne toast to our Big Day. Plus, they even came back to the hotel at 6:00 A.M. the next morning and chauffeured us to the airport to catch our honeymoon flight.

As Dawn, of Chicago, exclaims, "Boy, was this worth it!"

We shopped around for a deluxe "stretch" limousine. The prices of the rentals ranged from $25 to $150 per hour. There was usually a minimum rental time of three hours. This charge was based on a calculated amount of mileage. If, while renting, you exceeded that amount, an extra per-mile charge was applied. But boy, was it worth it! Our limo was a Rolls-Royce equipped with a stereo, a fully stocked service bar, a color television with a VCR, a moon roof, and books of matches with our name and wedding date engraved on them.

For an additional fee, some companies will even fill the vehicle with color-coordinated helium balloons that ascend around the bridal couple as the limousine door is opened for their ride to their reception site.

Karen, of Dover, Delaware, warns brides to be aware of limousine cancellation clauses.

Have you ever heard of a cancellation penalty for a limousine? Well, I didn't either, and after we contracted and paid a 50 percent ($75) deposit for the use of the limousine, a friend of my fiancé's offered, as his wedding gift to us, to drive us around in his Excalibur. This offer came ten days after we had signed the contract and a full month and a half before the wedding day. Our contract stated that we had five days to cancel to get a full refund. Since that time had passed, but it was still early enough for the limousine company to book other business, we were entitled to a 50 percent ($37.50) refund. Brides—read the small print. Ask what the cancellation policy is.

That story could only be topped by this one from Judy, of Crystal Lake, Illinois.

We contracted for our limousine four months before our wedding because we wanted to make sure we got their deluxe 15-foot "silver stretch" model. Our entire bridal party would fit inside, and we were excited about being able to be together to start off our celebration. What we didn't plan on was standing and waiting and waiting and waiting—the darn limo never showed up! The company had misplaced the order because it was made so far in advance, and they had forgotten about us. We got our full deposit back, but we never got what we wanted most—the luxury thrill ride.

It is also a good policy, throughout your wedding planning, to check with the Better Business Bureau to make sure that the company you are considering has never let anybody else down.

BRIDE BEWARE

When a limousine is reserved, a 50 percent deposit is required. The balance of the rental fee is collected when the limousine arrives at the pickup location. In addition, the driver collects a 15 percent gratuity at the final destination point.

If you are being driven to your ceremony in a friend or family member's car, Jodi, of Seattle, cautions you to consider the size of the vehicle.

I felt like a real queen in my beaded full white satin ball gown and my two-tier illusion veil. I was all ready to go as my uncle pulled up in his brand-new four-door sedan. I cringed when he opened the back door. Suddenly I knew what a sardine felt like. Not only did I feel like they had to pour me into it, I looked terrible with my train full of wrinkles.

If you have good friends who are special, but you cannot include them in the wedding party, they could play a great role by being your wedding chauffeurs as Kelly, of Chicago, suggests.

Two close friends of my husband's helped us tremendously by offering their services as official wedding chauffeurs. They provided their own cars and picked up, delivered, gave instructions, and even took our aunts and cousins on a mini tour of the city. They were fabulous! We sent each of them a special thank-you card with a certificate for a free wash and wax from the local car wash.

If family and friends are going to drive other guests to and from your wedding reception, it is a good idea to provide them with a list of who they are to pick up, the addresses of those people, the time of pickup, and the guests' phone numbers.

Ann, of Nashville, advises brides how to prevent any "get lost" possibilities.

One unhappy bride cried because the volunteer driver, who was chauffeuring the best man and other attendants, took the wrong exit and did not arrive at the reception dinner until dessert was being served.

The most important item to supply your appointed drivers with is a map showing directions from the ceremony site to the reception site—especially if it is located out of the city proper.

Unique methods of transportation are just as popular as luxurious modes, according to Carlene, of Tampa, Florida.

We wanted a limousine for our wedding but discovered it was just too much for our budget. As a great alternative idea, we rented a Lincoln Town Car for the entire day, and it only cost us $39.95. We got a special package that included unlimited mileage, and we felt like king and queen for the day.

Rates will vary in certain parts of the country. Each car rental company offers different car makes, and special promotions are usually offered periodically throughout the year. It is wise to call around for the best buy available. This type of luxury rental vehicle is a great idea.

Julie, of Tulsa, Oklahoma, suggests more ingenious modes of transportation.

My husband and I met on a commercial air flight en route to a business meeting. So when we decided to travel together forever, we planned an "airways" wedding. We rented an airplane. Both our families boarded with us including our minister. At 30,000 feet, with clear skies and no wind, we said our I dos.

Janice, of Houston, describes a unique wedding vehicle for 20 people.

We wanted our entire bridal party of 20 to be able to ride together, so we rented an antique red trolley car complete with a uniformed driver to transport all of us everywhere. The full day's rental cost us $100.

Susan, of St. Cloud, Minnesota, arranged for a caravan of '50s and '60s autos for her wedding party transportation.

Between the glistening chrome and the drivers in their blue jeans and black leather jackets, the cars were the perfect finish for our "oldie but goodie" theme wedding.

Mary, of Albuquerque, shares her nostalgic getaway idea.

We met in the park where we took our daily bike ride. After the ceremony on our June wedding day, we were literally joined together as we pedaled away on our bicycle built for two.

WEDDING LORE

A Slovak wedding ceremony was publicized by the arrival of the bride in a carriage drawn by six horses followed by a procession of her immediate family and bridesmaids.

If you're also a sentimentalist, consider using a horse and carriage or a classic antique auto for your getaway vehicle.

Although the cost of your wedding transportation should be limited to 3 percent of your total wedding budget, your vehicle choices, from antique cars to hot-air balloons, are as unlimited as your imagination.

CHAPTER 13

Other Wedding Parties

OTHER WEDDING PARTIES FACTS TO KNOW

1. Some Parties Are "For Ladies Only" while Others Are "For Men Only." Some Include Everyone.
2. Parties Can Range from an Informal Get-together to a Formal Sit-down Dinner.
3. Invitations for These Parties Can Be in the Form of a Telephone Invitation, an Informal Handwritten Note, or a Store-bought Preprinted Package.
4. Each Party Has Some Special Significance as Part of the Big Event of Your Wedding.
5. Food and Refreshments Are Usually Served.
6. Special Toasts and Gift Giving Are Usually Included as Part of These Parties.

Next to the wedding itself, most brides recall their bridal shower as being the most exciting event that took place during their wedding planning. Protocol for wedding showers and other prewedding parties is discussed in this chapter. Unique bridal luncheons and bachelor parties that build the momentum are also recounted. The rehearsal dinner, and the problems surrounding it, is also featured.

Sally, of Denver, describes her "purse" shower.

This was my second marriage. Between my husband and me, we have everything we needed. We decided to make it known that we preferred a "purse" shower, or wedding gifts of cash, and we told the members of our wedding party and our parents of this. They spread the word. As it turned out, our friends who attended our wedding were grateful because they were racking their brains trying to think of something for a "couple who has everything."

A special gift certificate, a check, a bond, or even a basket of coins can give a money gift a clever touch.

Jan, of San Diego, suggests the use of special registry "insert" cards.

My aunt hosted a bridal shower for me. To make it easier for my guests to learn what was on my "wedding wish list," the department store where I registered supplied pretty insert cards complete with their phone number that could be placed inside the shower invitations.

These practical ideas help your guests purchase gifts that you both want and will really appreciate.

Julie, of St. Louis, emphasizes the importance of a written thank you.

At my bridal shower when I opened each gift, I personally thanked the giver. In etiquette books, I had read that a thank-you note was not obligatory, so I felt I had done everything I needed to. *Wrong!* My aunts and the people who chipped in for the larger gifts were offended.

Thank-you notes are OBLIGATORY. *You must send notes of thanks for gifts that are received from people who did not attend*

EVERY BRIDE SHOULD KNOW ABOUT A TROUSSEAU:

A French word meaning "bundle," the trousseau was originally a bundle of clothing and personal possessions that the bride carried with her to her new home. Later the word was expanded to mean dowry, or all the things of value that a woman represented to attract prospective suitors.

the shower, as well as a separate thank you to each person who did attend and gave a gift or contributed to a joint gift.

Jean, of Paramus, New Jersey, describes her favorite shower gift.

One of the most romantic gifts I received for my bridal shower was a bridal veil plant. When I received it, this fernlike foliage was in full bloom with delicate tiny white blossoms that looked like a floral bridal veil.

Not only wedding guests can be invited to a bridal shower. One example is a bridal shower, or "toasting", given by your co-workers, club members, or school friends, where the get-together is really a break in the regular office or meeting routine. Their gift is usually one expression of affection for which everyone has chipped in. These participants need not be invited to your wedding and only one general thank-you card, posted where all can see it, is necessary.

Sharon, of Tulsa, Oklahoma, offers a money-saving shower tip.

I think every bride should make a point of inviting her bridesmaids to all of her showers but with the complete understanding that they are already giving their time, help, and money to pay for being a special part of her day. It also helps for the bride to let them know one small gift, if any, is all that should be considered. Announcing this when buying the dresses is a good time; it will clear the air and make everyone feel at ease about any additional obligations.

A special for-women-only party that honors the bridesmaids can be celebrated in many ways. Marny, of Toledo, explains that the idea of planning a special party for your bridesmaids is great, so long as it is not held early on the wedding day.

I made a big mistake that I want to warn other brides about. My wedding ceremony was planned for 4:00 P.M. In the morning, I had my nails and hair done. At noon, the bridesmaids gathered at my home where we held a special bridal luncheon. It did allow us to be together to eat something before the later activities and gave me a perfect opportunity to present their gifts to them and then to proceed to get dressed together for the ceremony. But it was too much with all that followed on that long, full day. By the time I arrived at my ceremony, I was tired and sorry that I had not allowed myself a more leisurely paced prewedding prep time.

Many brides also may not know that a bridesmaids' party may be large, including the bride, her attendants, both mothers, grandmothers, mothers of the children attendants, sisters, and sisters-in-law as well as any female relative or friend whom the bride wishes to invite. On the other hand, it can be as small as just the bride, her attendants, the two mothers, and the party hostess.

Laura, of Stamford, Connecticut, describes her bridesmaids' gathering.

I planned an All-American picnic at a local park and served hot dogs and potato salad on picnic tables with checkered tablecloths. I placed a rose at each bridesmaid's place, played my own wedding version of Trivial Pursuit, and even arranged for a singing telegram to be delivered by a "Teddy Bear Bride," who sang the praises of the bridesmaids. Of course, they took pictures to always remember this exciting and special party.

Tammi, of Charlotte, North Carolina, encourages all brides to treat their bridesmaids to a special party.

At my bridesmaid luncheon, held at a local restaurant, I really enjoyed the fun of supplying a centerpiece, placecards, and a wrapped gift for each attendant. My mother and I arrived early and were ready and waiting for them to arrive. For dessert, I even had a cake frosted with pink icing that contained a wedding ring. My younger sister got the piece with the ring in it. My mother, however, after seeing this, asked that she allow my dad and her a little time to catch their breath. My bridesmaids loved the party, and I feel that I included a very important part of planning a wedding.

* * *

> ### WEDDING LORE
>
> *Legend has it that bachelor parties were invented to raise a "fun fund" for the groom so he could carouse with his buddies even after his wife seized control of the household money.*

The boys night out is usually hosted by the best man or a friend or relative of the groom. Kevin, of Corpus Christi, Texas, describes the way his was celebrated.

Our state had recently legalized gambling, which allowed a dog racing track to operate. My best man arranged a novel bachelor party for me one evening at the race track. Our party of ten had reserved tables all set for dinner. Everyone received the evening's program and the announcer congratulated me over the loudspeaker by saying that because I only had a few days until post time and then my new wife, Natalie, would be taking over the reins, I was here to win a bundle to pay for the wedding. The "payout" was great, especially because we did win a trifecta bet that paid $750. The official results—it was a bachelor party that I'll never forget.

Mike, of Tampa, Florida, recalls how his groomsmen threw him into the back of a van and drove out of town to a secluded lake where they had rented a log cabin and stocked it with food, drinks, a television, VCR, and poker chips. They had a "sleepover" blast.

My bachelor party was a great last "single time" together for me and my early childhood pals, college roommates, and brothers. For me, the one thing that was so great about it was that there was no girl doing a striptease. Although my friends think that my morals belong back at the turn of the century, I feel that nudity is something between me and my wife. I would feel very self-conscious gawking at somebody's daughter gyrating for my pleasure. I decided to make this fact clear to my friends and they honored my wishes. It was as simple as that.

Telling the truth always turns out to be the best way to handle any situation. I'm sure this advice will encourage others who feel as you do.

Joe, of Detroit, explains the fallacy of the wild bachelor bash.

While most brides think that bachelor parties are an excuse for excessiveness that ends up at the county jail, the opposite is really the truth. To begin with, it is usually not a surprise because guys tend to let things go till the last minute and most often the groom hears them whispering about it. The evening begins with great enthusiasm, but after a few toasts and sports talk, total boredom begins to set in. Then someone gets a brilliant idea to go to topless bars. The bar is packed; it's smoky and the drinks are weak and expensive. The buddies want a "private dance" for the groom but are not able to gather together the excessive fee. The groom, looking annoyed, is breathing a sigh of relief at being able to avoid an embarrassing scene. By 1:00 A.M., everyone is yawning and ready to go home because they have to work the next day.

There is a certain bond between men that should never be lost. A bachelor party symbolizes the acceptance of a change that life has brought about. This is what makes the bachelor party an essential part of the nuptial rite of passage.

Jerry, of Boston, offers a great idea for getting home from the party safely.

My wife always thinks of everything. She not only surprised me with this, but showed me again how really smart she is. At about 1:00 A.M., a uniformed man appeared at our table at a local pub. He invited all of us to accompany him, as he had been appointed our official chauffeur. In front of the pub awaited a silver "stretch" limousine in which we drank a champagne toast to the bride and enjoyed a safe ride home.

No matter how tame they are, bachelor parties should always be held several days before the wedding in order to allow for recovery time.

Traditionally, the rehearsal dinner is held after the official rehearsal on the night before the wedding. However, if a morning ceremony is part of your plans, you may consider holding this special party a night or two before the rehearsal.

Michelle, of Kalistell, Minnesota, suggests another idea.

My husband's parents are deceased, so when we married, his godfather hosted our rehearsal dinner as a special wedding gift to us.

This gesture is highly commendable. It is also important to remember that while traditionally this party is hosted (paid for) by the groom's parents, it is not their responsibility—they do not have to do it! Actually, anyone who wants to can offer to give this party for the bridal couple.

Barb, of Springfield, Illinois, explains how she solved her rehearsal dinner problems.

For our rehearsal dinner, both space and money were limited. To solve this problem, we invited only those directly involved in the rehearsal, including our minister, to our private dinner party. At the same time, my aunt, my mother's only sister, hosted a snacks-and-refreshments party at her home for all of my out-of-town relatives. It really worked out very well.

It is only proper that if people from out-of-town are special enough to invite to your wedding, they should be invited to all of the parties relating to it as well.

The wedding rehearsal dinner is a great time to give a special thank-you gift to your attendants. A personal note with some special words of appreciation should be attached.

Debbie, of Austin, recalls how her rehearsal dinner was also a time for toasts.

The family and friends who made up our wedding party are fun-loving people. So on the occasion of our wedding rehearsal dinner, they gave my husband and me a mini "wedding roasting." Each person, including both mothers and fathers, had prepared a short story or tidbit about some experience we shared together. It was funny, it was touching, and it made that party the most memorable event surrounding our wedding day.

BRIDAL BARGAIN

Allow your in-laws to host your rehearsal dinner at their home. The savings on the food and refreshments as well as eliminating the clean-up at your parents' home immediately before the wedding are reasons enough to consider this helpful idea seriously. Besides, it allows the parents of the groom really to feel involved.

Kristin, of St. Louis, Missouri, describes a unique kind of wedding party.

I held a wedding work party at which a buffet supper, supplied by everyone bringing a dish, was served first, and followed by an evening of addressing invitations and making wedding favors.

Monica, of Rochester, New York, suggests another clever party idea.

My wedding day brunch for out-of-town guests was hosted by my aunt on the morning of my wedding. In this way, our family was welcomed and entertained while we, the bridal party and family, got ready for the ceremony.

Susan, of Billings, Montana, describes the "gift-opening party" held the day after her wedding.

Our wedding was held at a catering hall. We had a sizable amount of food left so my parents decided to invite the wedding party and immediate family to their house (my old home) for a gift-opening party. My husband and I had spent the night in a honeymoon suite at a hotel and were not leaving for our honeymoon until that next evening. Around noon, everyone arrived and snacked on leftovers, reminisced about the wedding day, and watched as my husband and I opened our gifts. It was great because it gave my grandparents another chance to visit with the family before they returned to their retirement home in Arkansas later that day. Actually, my parents drove my grandparents and my husband and me to the airport that evening where we finally ended a memorable family event.

Joann, of New Orleans, suggests another clever "after-the-wedding" party idea.

Have you heard of a thank-you party? Although it's not required, it's a lovely gesture to invite everyone who helped to make your wedding successful to be the first guests in your new home. We not only held our first dinner party, but also entertained everyone with our wedding and honeymoon pictures and our

---

BRIDE BEWARE

The old rule that a relative should never give a shower has faded into oblivion. There is no reason why a loving aunt or cousin cannot entertain for the bride. Immediate family, however—mothers and sisters—still do not give showers, as this makes them appear greedy.

wedding video. It was an extraspecial way of showing our thoughtfulness and appreciation.

Traditional prewedding parties should not take up more than 5 percent of your wedding budget. Do make every effort to include as many of these extraspecial parties as possible. They provide specific opportunities for the expression of love and joy for the bride, groom, and all who are a part of their happiness.

CHAPTER 14

Gifts

GIFT FACTS TO KNOW

1. A Gift Registry Is a Free Service that Enables Guests to Learn What You Would Like Most for a Wedding Gift.
2. Register Immediately After You Become Engaged so that Guests Can Get Gift Ideas for the Other Wedding Parties as Well.
3. Register at Several Places to Allow Your Guests Wide Price and Gift Choices.
4. It Is Proper to Acknowledge Each Gift with a Written Thank-you Note of Appreciation.
5. It Is Customary to Give Attendants a Thank-you Gift.
6. Attendant Gifts May Be Identical or Individual.
7. If a Wedding Is Temporarily Postponed, All Gifts Are Kept.
8. If a Wedding Is Canceled, All Gifts *Must* Be Returned with a Note of Explanation.

This chapter is about the protocol of gift giving and receiving. It discusses unique gift registries and the etiquette of exchanging wedding gifts. Problems with damaged gifts, when and how wedding gifts should be returned, and most of all, the importance of sending prompt thank-you notes are featured.

Amy, of Davenport, Iowa, explains that a bridal registry can work well for both the bridal couple and their guests if some important steps are followed.

I registered eight months before my wedding. We got what we wanted without having to exchange *anything*. Not only were our gifts useful, we also got them in the colors we wanted.

Some brides may not realize it, but registering for bridal gifts is a free service. You are free to register at as many places as you feel are affordable and convenient for your guests.

It is a statistical fact that brides purchase one-half of all of the tabletop (china, crystal, and silverware) sold annually in the United States. Today china pieces harmonize rather than match, and crystal is used for every meal.

Carol, of Princeton, New Jersey, recommends using a registry.

I would suggest that all brides register at least three months before their wedding date, so that people invited to the shower can know what they would like. The store I registered at even supplied my bridal shower hostess with cards that she inserted into the shower invitations so people could call there easily. About 80 percent of my guests used the registry.

In contrast, Nancy, of Pittsburgh, wasn't so lucky.

Only 20 percent of my shower gifts were things I registered for. But perhaps that was because I waited until one week before my shower to register.

Melissa, of Baltimore, discovered a gracious answer.

My bridal registrar suggested a very gracious and tactful way to answer everyone who asked what I wanted for my wedding. Whenever the question was put to me, I would reply "Tom and I are registered at Macy's. You might find something you like there as much as we do."

Today the wedding registry extends far beyond the traditional department store. Other options include:

- HARDWARE STORE registries that offer lawn and garden equipment, power tools, decorating supplies, and household accessories—practical and functional necessities of home-ownership.
- MORTGAGE COMPANIES now offer home mortgage registries into which guests may deposit monetary contributions for a couple's down payment.
- HIGH-TECH APPLIANCES are the number-one choice for busy working couples who want and need items such as a food processor, a slow cooker, and easy-care cookware to make their lives easier.
- TRAVEL AGENCIES offer honeymoon registries to allow guests to supply a champagne dinner for you, a day of deep-sea fishing, or tickets to a Broadway show—all of which make the couple's honeymoon that much more special.
- TRADITIONAL REGISTRIES that specialize in tabletop essentials now offer china, crystal, and silver at 50 percent savings along with catalogs and 800 numbers for easy gift registering and purchasing.

Although money is the number-one gift item given to a wedding couple, it is the one gift that a bride should **never** *ask for personally. The mother of the bride, the maid of honor, or other close family members can easily get this message across. Money can be given in several forms. They include: Personal checks/special gift checks/store gift certificates/U.S. Savings Bonds/stock certificates.*

Vickie, of Topeka, Kansas, suggests a novel way money gifts may be stored.

My maid of honor gave me an unusual bridal ensemble consisting of a blue garter, a new pair of white lace hosiery, an old coin (for good luck), and she lent me her bridal purse. It was a beautiful drawstring satin bag that measured 9 by 12 inches and was trimmed with lace. I carried it on my wedding day and safely stored in it all of the envelopes we received from our guests. That evening, after the reception, my husband and I opened our cards. As we did this, we endorsed our money gifts officially as "Mr. and Mrs." and added FOR DEPOSIT ONLY under our names. My dad then deposited them for us after we left for our honeymoon.

Another helpful idea is to write the amount and form of money (Example: Gift Certificate) inside each card as you read it. When writing your thank-you notes, you'll be happy you jotted it down.

Bob, of Trenton, New Jersey, who, like many other grooms, shared in the expense of his wedding, wanted a voice in how their money was being spent. His wife, Mary, gives the background.

My husband and I were 28 years old when we married. We both had lived on our own and had previously shopped for our own home merchandise. He has his own taste and style and really enjoyed selecting items with me that we would both use and live with. I even learned something new about him—how he has always hated the color green. We really had a fun time registering together and it got us excited about starting our new life.

Men of the '90s are, more than ever, taking an active interest in their personal lives. This is especially true if they have lived on their own or are combining households.

Statistics show that 85 percent of remarried brides bring their future husbands in with them to register rather than their mothers.

> WEDDING LORE
>
> *In the early 1900s newspapers often printed a list of requested gifts, including china and silver patterns, as part of each wedding announcement. Sometime between World War I and World War II, the practice was formally dubbed the bridal registry and large department stores began to offer it as a service.*

Brenda, of Akron, Ohio, asks if you have ever considered insuring your wedding gifts.

My uncle, an insurance agent, gave us a unique bridal shower gift. It was an insurance policy that covered all of the gift items we would receive as well as my diamond engagement ring. If anything would have been lost or stolen, it was completely covered. The policy was a type of renter's insurance that covered a six-month time period and could be renewed if we so desired.

Agnes, the grandmother of a bride in San Antonio, recalls giving a cherished wedding gift.

I was in a difficult position. I had some rare pieces of silver that had been in our family for two generations. My granddaughter, however, lives in jeans and eats off of paper plates. I was afraid to give these very precious keepsakes to someone who wouldn't really appreciate them. My son suggested a solution. I invited her to my home and brought out the set of silver for her to see. I told her of its history, its meaning, and asked her if she would like to carry on the tradition. She really surprised me by saying that she loved antique items and would cherish it as her favorite wedding gift.

If she had not reacted with this enthusiasm, you could have easily saved it for another family member, knowing that you had made the appropriate gestures.

Today brides can roam through a department store using a hand-held portable scanner that enters their gift choices into the store's registry computer much like a grocery store checks out food items.

Transmitting this "wedding wish list" into the computer does not always guarantee a problem-free system, as Connie, of Evanston, Illinois, explains.

I thought that a computerized registry automatically removes gifts as they are purchased, thus eliminating duplicate gifts. I registered at a major department store, yet I received three irons. One of them was damaged in shipment. I returned the damaged gift in its original packing material. They were happy to replace

---

BRIDAL BARGAIN

Ask your parents to check with their agent about a "floater" policy on their homeowner's insurance. This will provide inexpensive protection of your wedding gifts from the time of their arrival through your honeymoon.

it, allow me to exchange it for another different gift, or refund the money—it was up to me.

Reputable stores will gladly replace a damaged item with no hassle. Duplicate items can also be returned or exchanged. However, without evidence that you are registered at that store, or without a receipt, the store will only give you credit for the recent "sale price" of that item. It is not appropriate to notify givers about duplicate gifts. Simply send a gracious note of thanks for their thoughtfulness.

Audrey, of Des Moines, Iowa, is an experienced wedding guest with a "duplicate gift" solution.

I realize that in spite of good record keeping, mistakes can happen and things do get overlooked. As an aunt and a great-aunt, I have attended many showers and weddings. I have made it a practice to include a tiny card taped to the inside cover of the gift box that tells that the gift is from me, along with the date and the store location that I purchased it at.

Some department stores enclose a decorative sticker inside the box cover. It includes the store name, department number, and the purchase date. In addition, many stores will also gift-wrap the present and send it directly to the bride's home.

A bridal registry is only as good as the person who punches in the order, as Judy, of Richmond, Virginia, illustrates.

When I married recently, I invited a good friend from college. For our gift, she ordered two fine crystal goblets from my registry. However, I received six goblets. I was overwhelmed by this expensive gift and called her. My friend, billed triple what she expected, graciously told us to keep them. My husband felt obligated and investigated this matter. My friend had 60 days to legally contest the billing error according to the Federal Trade Commission. If the error was an honest shipping mistake, I could have returned the merchandise making the store pay for the postage and handling. If after 30 days the store did not pick up the goblets or refused to pay for the return mail expenses, I had the right to keep the $150 gift without cost.

Carolyn, of Lincoln, Nebraska, explains her registry hassles.

I'm convinced that stores don't remove items just to get more sales. I received 12 place settings of the formal china I selected and registered for. Shortly before the wedding, another eight place settings arrived. I returned them immediately, but the store would not give me a credit outside of the gift registry department. I had to bring in all of the receipts from the extra place settings I received. I proved that they failed to log the purchases. The bottom line—save all your receipts!

My best advice is to follow up. Check your registry for errors. All changes usually take three to five days to enter locally throughout a city. For other states, it may take up to two weeks.

Joan, of Burbank, California, warns brides to check receipts and labels.

Be sure to also check gifts against receipts. When I received a box and the shipping label said box 2 of 2, I was confused. I never received another box, and if I hadn't looked on the label, I would not have known there was another one. The first box never was found, but I did get a refund.

Susan, of Spokane, gives this advice.

I received a beautiful crystal cake plate, and the card with the gift was positively illegible. I called the store from which the gift was shipped. They kept records at the store and were able to supply the name of the purchaser, who turned out to be my father's boss.

Kathy, of Newark, was puzzled about a "lost" gift.

During a conversation with a close friend, she mentioned that she had sent me a wedding gift. Several weeks passed and there was still no sign of it. While I realized that the store might have misplaced it or it might have gotten lost in the mail, I was too embarrassed to ask her outright about it.

Don't be embarrassed! Eventually she will ask you if you received it, because she did not receive a thank-you note which is usually sent no later than thirty days after the wedding. According

BRIDE BEWARE

Some stores claim they will send your guests a computer printout upon request. Test this by asking for one under your sister's name.

to protocol, a wedding guest has up to one year to send a wedding gift.

Jennifer, of Ann Arbor, asks, "how considerate are you?"

It is easy to get caught up in the excitement and hustle-bustle of wedding planning. When several gifts arrived and my husband had to inform me that they were from his family members, I realized that his parents were probably also unaware of some of these gifts, so I invited them over to see the gifts and go over our plans as they were being finalized. The little time that this took was well worth it. Not only were warm family ties created, their visit dissolved any resentment and embarrassment they may have had by their not knowing what was received and by whom.

Chris, of Louisville, Kentucky, warns . . .

Never, I mean never, open your gifts at your reception! It was a disaster. After our honeymoon, only one week later, I didn't remember which gift came from whom.

Not only is it a mistake to open gifts, it is a mistake for guests to bring gifts to a wedding reception. Bridal registries suggest that all wedding gifts be sent **before** *the wedding day, to the bride, at the address listed on the wedding invitation. If guests decide to bring box gifts or envelope gifts, be sure that some family member or close friend has been delegated to move them unopened from the reception site to a safe place, until you return from your honeymoon.*

A major credit card company's survey determined that people spend an average of $68 on a wedding gift. Forty-eight percent of those interviewed considered shopping for wedding gifts a difficult task. Why? Forty-five percent feared "looking cheap."

Marriage manners dictate that it is improper to ask your guests where they purchased your gift, as Cheryl, of Annapolis, Maryland, explains.

I was very careful about registering for only those items that I really wanted. In spite of that, I received gifts I really didn't want. I know that it is impolite to ask someone to exchange the gift they gave you. And because I didn't want the giver to know I exchanged their present, I just took it back myself, quietly, and never mentioned that I didn't like it, or that it was one of several I received.

This bride was using appropriate wedding manners. It is, after all, the thought that counts. Your guests spent time and thought selecting a special gift for you. Even if it isn't the present of your dreams, it still deserves an expression of appreciation.

Paula, of Albany, listened to her mother's advice.

I received many lovely gifts from my bridal shower as well as my wedding. I personally thanked everyone and thought that I could buy a preprinted thank-you card at a stationery store. My mother questioned my intentions and urged me to send a note to everyone concerned.

Your mother is absolutely right. If you decided to have a wedding celebration, you automatically must accept the responsibility of personally writing a note of thanks and appreciation for every gift you receive—no matter how small. The only verbal thank-you that is proper is for a wedding telegram. It is also easier if you send the thank-yous as you receive the gifts—or you may never catch up.

For the special people who made your wedding the wonderful event it was, special consideration is in order, as Kathy, of Fulton, Maryland, explains.

Many people helped me make my wedding a memorable occasion. I wanted them to know that I had not overlooked or forgotten their special efforts. I arranged to have floral bouquets sent to both sets of parents a few days after the wedding while we were on our honeymoon. With the flowers, I included a special personal note to them thanking them for making our beautiful wedding possible. My mother tells me how she reads my words of love and appreciation over and over again.

Patricia, of Chicago, had her wedding mementos engraved.

I wanted to give my attendants something special. I was told that their gifts could be identical, or the bridesmaids could get the same items and the honor attendants could receive a special gift.

MOST WANTED
WEDDING GIFTS

Annually, I conduct a national survey of brides and major registries across America to discover what items are most desirable on their gift wish list. Currently, these are the top ten.

1. A Down comforter
2. Classic tabletop
   a. Fine china
   b. Crystal
   c. Silver holloware
3. VCR
4. Microwave oven
5. Food processor
6. Vacuum cleaner
7. Cutlery
8. Coffeemaker
9. Slow cooker/toaster
10. Cookware

I decided on the same gift for everyone that would be engraved with their names and our wedding date as a lasting memento. Places like Things Remembered have a huge selection of gift ideas for this kind of purchase.

You might also consider sending a special short note when you return from your honeymoon to express your appreciation for those sharing in this most memorable event. The note can recall a funny wedding day happening or it can reflect on what their relationship means to you.

Jerry, of Cape Cod, describes how he honored his bride with a special wedding gift.

I gave my wife a special gift on our wedding day. It was a charm bracelet with a wedding bell charm attached to it that really rang. I even had our initials engraved on the bell. I also wrote a short poem to her and included it with the gift. It became a keepsake gift to which I intend to keep adding important remembrances. She just loved it, and maybe other brides might feel the same.

There is no rule about wedding couples exchanging gifts but many do. It is usually a useful item that has sentimental value and will be treasured for years to come.

The day you announce your wedding date, expect gifts to start arriving. Your guests want to share in your happiness, and do so by giving you gifts. While marriage manners dictate that a handwritten personal note of thanks be sent for each gift received, there is no reason why your groom can't assist you with this duty.

Encore Weddings

ENCORE WEDDING FACTS TO KNOW

1. An Engagement Ring Is Appropriate, but an Engagement Announcement Is Not Necessary.
2. Most Encore Wedding Couples Pay for Their Own Weddings.
3. Your Children Should Be Included in Any Way Possible.
4. Civil and Nonsectarian Are the Most Popular Encore Ceremony Choices.
5. The Only Required Attendants Are Honor Attendants.
6. The Bride Can Definitely Wear White.
7. An Intimate Reception Party with an Average of 50 to 100 Family and Close Friends Is Customary.
8. A Bridal Shower Is Perfectly Acceptable.
9. All Traditional Wedding Customs Are Appropriate—Throwing the Bouquet Is Optional.
10. Ex-spouses Are Usually Not Invited.

Forty-nine percent of the 2.5 million marriages that take place annually in the United States are remarriages. This chapter lists the basic protocol of an "encore" wedding which can be twice as wonderful with both feet on the ground. Specific topics such as ex-spouses, in-laws, and involvement of children in the wedding are featured. Etiquette ideas for the encore wedding reception are also highlighted.

The greatest joy of remarriage is the opportunity for a second chance at love, as Linda, of Rochester, Minnesota, explains.

I'm so happy to be living in the '90s. In earlier generations, most women stayed in bad marriages because they didn't have the social support of dating services or the financial opportunity for a career of their own. I'm glad I was able to once again enjoy the "singles scene," but I'm happy to have kissed it good-bye for the right partner, with whom I can feel at ease and truly compatible. I have chosen this one for better, deeper reasons and without any rose-colored glasses. So, if you're getting ready to take the plunge once more, get ready to enjoy. The best is yet to come.

Michelle, of Knoxville, Tennessee, had an unusual twist to her encore wedding.

My husband and I were married and divorced several years ago. We will be married again this week. We discussed this unusual situation with several local bridal advisors and consulted an etiquette book and a local librarian. The final decision was to have a very simple quiet ceremony followed by a very special romantic honeymoon. We felt that a formal printed announcement of our remarriage was not fitting. Rather, we purchased some elegant prepackaged note cards and sent a personalized notice only to those acquaintances and business associates that we felt needed to be informed of our new status.

Under the circumstances, you not only got a lot of knowledgeable advice, but your actions were very appropriate.

Barbara, of Wichita, Kansas, included generations of family in her second wedding.

My husband's grandson and my granddaughter introduced us a few years ago. On our wedding day, my grown married son gave me away. We beamed as we said "I do," reflecting on how it took over 55 years before love had connected us.

From the moment two people say "I do," their obligations to each other and society begin to grow. Laws exist to ensure equal rights, privileges, and marital stability.

Here's an original idea from Donna, of Scranton, Pennsylvania, regarding prenuptial agreements, which seem to arise more frequently with encore weddings.

My husband and I are working professionals. We each own a condo and a car. We looked at our prenuptial agreement as a security blanket intended to provide necessary flexibility for our modern marriage. The greatest part about it is that after five years, it will expire automatically. Circumstances change, children are born, and our marital roles will be altered. We feel that this clause not only recognizes these changes, but more than that, it affirms our belief in a lasting marriage.

Unfortunately, most people don't bother about laws until difficulties arise. Then often it is too late to benefit from the protection the laws afford. Thus, learn all you can about the laws of marriage before the ceremony. This is not unromantic; we love with our heads as well as our hearts.

Elizabeth, of Vail, Colorado, tells her uplifting story.

I had been married and divorced three times. I was fifty years old. I had made up my mind to spend the rest of my life as a single woman. But fate had other plans for me. I met my husband on an airplane. We were married almost a year to the day after our meeting. We had a lovely dinner party at a resort with 50 friends and relatives. Our dinner place cards were airplane-shaped cookie cutters with luggage tags attached. I guess the message is— it is never too late for love.

BRIDE BEWARE

If you are planning to change your name officially after your encore wedding, you must repeat the process of filing appropriate legal forms for all of the necessary documents.

More than 75 percent of those divorced or widowed remarry within five years. Most couples pay for their own second weddings, which can be whatever kind of celebration fits their lifestyle and their pocketbook.

Lynn, of Clearwater, Florida, says:

My first wedding was videotaped. I recorded my second wedding right over it.

For her encore wedding, Connie, of Corpus Christi, Texas, felt that her personal preference was more important than etiquette.

Years ago, my father escorted me down the aisle. He is still living, but I was now a grown woman with a child and I did not want to redo my first wedding. Instead, my new husband and I walked down the aisle in front of all our family and friends to symbolize that we had come here openly, freely and together.

Many encore brides are incorporating their own special symbolism into their ceremonies and their receptions. One rule covers this—there is no one rule anymore.

Angela, of Boulder, Colorado, who didn't want to mix orange blossoms with crow's feet, had this remarriage solution.

I was very undecided about what kind of dress I should wear for my second wedding. After all, I was 39 years old and had two growing children. The informal bridal gowns seemed too elaborate. My salesclerk had a marvelous idea. She brought out several bridesmaid dresses that were definitely less formal looking, yet very beautiful. I didn't even know you could order a bridesmaid dress in white or ivory. The dresses ranged from $75 to $150, so it was a great buy in more ways than one.

If you had a large wedding the first time, there is a general rule of thumb that says you should think twice about wearing an elaborate white wedding gown, unless you are still fairly young and childless.

THE WORLD'S RECORD HOLDERS FOR THE MOST MARRIAGES

The greatest number of monogamous marriages recorded by one man is 27. His name is Glynn "Scotty" Wolfe, born July 25, 1908. His first marriage occurred in 1927. His current wife is Daisy Delgado, born December 9, 1970. His total number of children is, he believes, 41. For a woman, the greatest number of monogamous marriages is 21. She is Linda Lou Essex of Anderson, Indiana. She has been married to 15 different men since 1957, divorcing the last one in 1988.

—Guinness Book of World Records

Jodi, of Queens, New York, emphasized the blending of families in her encore ceremony.

When my husband and I planned our wedding (the second for both of us), we researched ways to include my daughter and his two sons in our ceremony. I saw an advertisement for medallions for the blended family. I sent for them. We also asked our pastor about what we could do to include a special ceremony focusing on the family nature of marriage. He had heard of the medallions and worked with us to include a unique ceremony within the ceremony. After we exchanged our rings, the children walked up to the altar together. My husband and I placed a medallion around the neck of each child while we pledged to love and care for them. It really made the merging of our families official, and it turned out to be a very important step in building our relationship as one unit.

You can also create your own family ceremony by using unique tokens or symbols, such as a cross or good-luck charm, that has a special meaning to all of you.

Cathryn, of Fort Myers, Florida, even included the children at the engagement party.

My children, each wearing a flower and a name badge, greeted guests as they arrived and took their coats. They also helped by serving refreshments and passing out appetizers among their soon-to-be new family members. They really felt important and it was a novel way for my husband's family to get to know them.

When children are very young, they may not fully comprehend a family service, but they will understand when someone conveys a message of love, as Susan, of Newark, explains.

My seven-year-old daughter was apprehensive about my marriage to my second husband. I had been divorced for four years, and she alone had been the center of my world. Her attitude changed dramatically after we included her in our wedding ceremony. During it we placed a special gold cross on a chain around her neck. My daughter told everyone that she got it because we

---

BRIDAL BARGAIN

Consider wearing your mother's wedding dress for your second wedding. It could be cut to tea length and tinted either pale blue, peach, or pink. This allows for a unique blending of something traditional and something contemporary.

think she is very special, and she fondly remembers our wedding as "the day *we* got married together."

Christine, of Baton Rouge, Louisiana, offers another unique way to include the children.

We included all five children of our combined families by mentioning each child by name in our program and including a short message that each child had personally written about their thoughts on beginning our new life together.

Mary, of Grayslake, Illinois, recalls her special ceremony within the ceremony.

Our pastor included a special blessing at the end of our ceremony that was very touching. With my husband and me standing before him, he called each of "our" four children forward by name. The first (oldest) child approached and stood between us, taking our hands. The second followed, taking her brother and my husband's hand. The third came up and stood between her brother and sister followed by the fourth, completing a linked half circle around the pastor. He then asked God's special blessing on not only our marriage but, more important, our family. It was very touching.

Couples can also include children in their ceremony by allowing them to participate in the unity candle lighting.

Annette, of Macon, Georgia, describes a tradition she and her husband began on their wedding day.

We started a tradition on our wedding day that will reemphasize our commitment to our family for many years. We gave each of our children an engraved silver goblet with their name and our wedding date on it. At Christmas and on each anniversary, we will drink together from these cups to celebrate and continue our family ritual. As new family members are added or born into our family, they too will be given their special goblet.

These stories all reflect the general consensus that while a bride and her mother usually plan the first wedding, it is the bride and groom, and their children, who should plan the second.

WEDDING LORE

Insure the success of your encore marriage by wedding on December 31, the luckiest day of the year, according to the Irish. Carry a horseshoe decorated with flowers and four-leaf clovers for luck, and be sure to put a lucky sixpence in your shoe.

Rachel, of Montreal, California, explains what to do with ex-spouses and former in-laws.

I was divorced but had a friendly arrangement with my former husband. I am also still very close to my former in-laws. To make my son happy, I invited both my ex-husband and in-laws to my second wedding. I realize that it is better not to do this, but it actually worked out quite well. They were seated with our neighbors, and I simply introduced my "ex" as Jerry's father and my ex-mother-in-law as his grandmother.

If you do not have a friendly situation, avoid this completely. It could have been a painfully awkward occasion.

Beth, of Kokoma, Indiana, describes a different kind of in-law dilemma.

My husband had died, suddenly, about one year ago. I met another man and we were just married. We were both very concerned about how my family, especially my former in-laws, whom I am still close to, would react. We included my two young daughters as junior bridesmaids. The most endearing person at our wedding was our minister. His moving words compared me to a desert, alone and barren with my loss, and he talked about how life can flower again with my newfound happiness. If there had been any doubt in anyone's mind, these spirited words changed them.

Gwen, of Cicero, Illinois, offers some practical etiquette advice.

I have been married and divorced twice. My husband was never married. Although many of the same people who attended my first wedding were also invited to this one, I chose to have a medium-size wedding (100 people) complete with a pale-pink floor-length gown and all the traditional customs because my husband deserved the right to a "real" wedding once in his life too.

Whether this is your second, third, or fourth marriage, this is still the "first" of your new partnership together. This decision was not only considerate, it was also the appropriate solution.

Combine contemporary with traditional, as Margo, of Ames, Iowa, did.

I had a very unusual cake for my second wedding. It stood upright on the table and was shaped into a giant number "2." It had the traditional cake-topper figurines of a bride and groom and was beautifully decorated with frosting flourishes. Everyone thought it was very clever. Our guests kept asking us if we were trying to prove that "love is better the second time around," or was it that our second marriage was going to be "twice as sweet!"

Lucy, of Mankato, Minnesota, provided a favorite poem given to her as a framed embroidered keepsake to hang in her new home:

Love is a circle.
The more you do for a man, the more he loves you. The more
he loves you, the more he tries to do for you. The more he
tries to do for you, the more you love him. And so it goes.
—Anonymous

Anita, of Trenton, New Jersey, verifies that happiness can be had the second time around.

My second wedding was ten times better than my first because I did it my own way. We had a smaller, more elegant affair. We invited 35 people and served them a fancy sit-down dinner. I wore a crystal-blue cocktail suit, cut my wedding cake, and even threw my nosegay bouquet as we ran to our limousine to catch the airplane for our weekend honeymoon in Las Vegas. Everything was perfect. I would not have done it any other way.

Shelly, of El Paso, was quoted:

Only now, after having a second chance, can I honestly say that I had a perfect wedding.

It is also noteworthy that an encore couple take the time for a honeymoon. This special time together, however short it may have to be, is necessary to make new memories together.

America is truly a melting pot for marriage. Mixed marriages, second marriages, interfaith marriages, even remarriage to your former husband are all perfectly acceptable and appropriate "love matches" in the '90s.

CHAPTER 16

The Honeymoon

HONEYMOON FACTS TO KNOW

1. Always Work Through a Professional Travel Agent for the Best Information on the Newest Facilities and the Greatest Buys.
2. Honeymoons Can Be Any Kind of Getaway.
3. "All-inclusive" Resorts Where Everything Is Included for One Price Offer Real Value.
4. Cruises Offer a Unique Floating City of Fun and Excitement.
5. Arrangements Must Be Made if Passports Are Needed.

Typically, after the year-long planning of a perfect day, the average couple looks forward to a little time alone, with all the worries of the wedding behind them. In this chapter, basic honeymoon planning details are listed. You will read about the comedies and tragedies of getting away. Couples' experiences with disappointing "dream vacations" that ended up being too long, too short, or too far away are described. Also featured are unusual wedding night tales that will guide couples in making their arrangements fool-proof.

Kim, of Las Vegas, suggests "free" honeymoon guidance.

My best advice to a wedding couple is to work with and through a competent travel agent. There is no charge to the bridal couple for this service, as the travel agent earns a commission from the airline and hotel into which they book you. These agents are usually well traveled and know about every new resort that exists, as well as all of the resort's amenities.

The most important paper you need with you on your honeymoon is your written hotel confirmation. It should specify all of the details such as your room rate, guaranteed dates of occupancy, and all special services that are to be included in the rate.

Holly, of Atlanta, offers a few words about your honeymoon wardrobe.

I would advise every bride to go through all of the clothes she is planning to take with her on her honeymoon and put half of them away. We went to Jamaica on our honeymoon and almost all of the time we were there, we wore our bathing suits and shorts and T-shirts. We really didn't need several changes of clothes each day. I would, however, highly recommend some enticing undergarments if you want to spice up your honeymoon.

A cruise can be an ocean of fun. No waiting, no theater lines, no dinner reservations necessary. There's no doubt about it, a honeymoon cruise is different and exciting. You'll never be hungry, and especially with a DO NOT DISTURB sign on your door, it is definitely as romantic as Brenda, of Altoona, Pennsylvania, reports.

We went on a honeymoon cruise. It was so romantic and relaxing, I would recommend that every bride and groom, especially second-marriage couples as we were, look into this. The walks on the deck in the moonlight, our cozy private cabin, the fabulous unending amount of food, and every possible activity, including a masquerade ball, made it a "dream" honeymoon. It was especially fun because five of the six couples at our table were also on their honeymoons. It was interesting to compare the customs and types of weddings that each couple, from all different parts of America, celebrated on the same wedding day.

A cruise is also ALL-INCLUSIVE! That means everything— all food, beverages, your cabin, gratuities and all activities on ship are included in the one price you pay for the cruise. Cruise ships go everywhere around the world. Trips range from three days (approximately $600 per person) to 14 days (approximately $1,995 per person). This also includes your airfare from your town to the port where the ship leaves from.

For a thrilling honeymoon, Sharon, of Nashville, advises brides to consider train travel.

Experienced travel agents suggest this travel option for honeymooners. Your very own private compartment, breathtaking landscapes, and ever-changing scenery are just the beginning. Unique theme trains, like a restored 1920's train, or the European Express, which travel agents tell honeymooners to think of as a cruise by rail, offer couples elaborate, exquisite pampering. Train honeymoons can range from 24 hours to as long as two weeks. They run across America as well as Europe. Local travel agents can give you full details and glamorous brochures.

According to a national travel newsletter's survey of frequent travelers:

MOST ROMANTIC U.S. HIDEAWAYS	MOST ROMANTIC WORLD HIDEAWAYS

Bel-Air Hotel
  Los Angeles, California
	Hotel San Pietro
	  Positano, ITALY

Stonepipe
  Carmel Valley, California
	Amanpuri
	  Phuket Island, THAILAND

Most Romantic
U.S. Hideaways (cont.)

Hana-Maui Beach
    Maui, Hawaii
Mansion on Turtle Creek
    Dallas, Texas
Mauna Lani Bay
    Hawaii's Big Island
Sherman House
    San Francisco, California
San Ysidro Ranch
    Montecito, California
Kona Village
    Hawaii's Big Island
Lowell Hotel
    New York City, New York
Ritz Carlton
    Laguna Niguel, California
Four Seasons Clift
    San Francisco, California
Highlands Inn
    Carmel, California

Most Romantic
World Hideaways (cont.)

Park Hotel Vitznau
    Vitznau, SWITZERLAND
Hotel Cipriani
    Venice, ITALY
Chateau d'Esclimont
    St. Symphorien, FRANCE
Cap Julica
    Anguilla, BRITISH WEST
    INDIES
El Minzah Hotel
    Tangier, MOROCCO
Mauna Kea Beach Hotel
    Hawaii's Big Island
The Connaught
    London, ENGLAND
The Regent
    Hong Kong
Las Hadas
    Manzanillo, MEXICO
Le Manoir aux Quat'Saisons
    Oxford, ENGLAND

Cara, of Brooklyn, suggests a honeymoon "survival" kit.

World travelers recommend that on all vacations, travelers should not forget to take along small packets of spot remover, nail polish remover, and a small bottle of liquid detergent. No mishaps should ruin an otherwise relaxing honeymoon. They were absolutely right.

A small first aid kit is also a necessity. Stock it with the basics—antiseptic, aspirin, Pepto-Bismol, and Band-Aids.

If you are planning a honeymoon trip that will require you to have a passport, listen to these words of advice from Danielle, of Joliet, Illinois.

My husband surprised me by announcing that he had booked a trip to Jamaica for us for our honeymoon. I was flabber-

---

BRIDE BEWARE

Certain months during the year are considered the "peak season." Cruise ships, resorts, and hotels get premium rates that are two or three times as expensive as off-peak seasons. Be sure to check the yearly rate schedules for the dates you are considering. A weekend getaway honeymoon is an alternate way to save money. Many resorts and hotels offer fabulous romantic weekend packages.

gasted. However, in all of the excitement of the wedding planning, we overlooked the fact that our passports had to be applied for eight to 12 weeks in advance of the trip. We discovered this one month before the wedding. Luckily, there are passport services such as the Center for International Business and Travel (CIBT). Even though the charges for the passports were $20 more than the regular $45 charge we would have paid if we got them at the post office, they were delivered in one week and saved our honeymoon.

Brides and grooms should also know that passports are valid for ten years. The number for the CIBT is 800-424-2429.

Want to know what the weather will be like at your honeymoon destination? American Express now offers a 900-weather number that gives you tips about traveling and tipping as well as an up-to-the-minute and around-the-clock weather report from every major city in the world.

Roseann, of Ames, Iowa, describes a honeymoon custom that provided a special homecoming.

An old American custom tells how neighbors and friends would keep evil spirits away by serenading the newlyweds on their return from the honeymoon with the banging of noisemakers. This was known as a shivaree. When my husband and I returned from our honeymoon in the Poconos, we were put in a crate and pulled around the countryside from 9:00 P.M. to 11:00 P.M. Then the shivaree organizers moved the party to a local tavern for drinks.

This ritual also symbolizes the uniting of two different "kins" and is actually a fertility ritual. Other shivaree ideas include a welcome-home picnic or a moonlight ride in the park.

Great escapes should not put you in great debt. **Ways to get the best honeymoon buys are:**

1. Work with a travel agency that has a wedding registry. In that way, guests can make gift donations toward your trip.

WEDDING LORE

It is said that couples honeymooning in Niagara Falls will have good fortune if they remember to toss pennies in the Bridal Veil Falls.

2. Consider a prepackaged tour that is all-inclusive—
   INCLUDES EVERYTHING—for one price.
3. Travel off-season.
4. Book reservations through clubs or organization
   memberships such as AAA or the Amoco Motor Club
   for additional discounts on airfare, rental cars, and hotels.
   For maximum savings, reserve all of these things at
   one time.

Always use and carry traveler's checks, and only small amounts of cash. Sign traveler's checks only in front of the authorized agent who is cashing them. **Other important papers to remember to take with you are:**

1. Driver's license
2. Marriage license
3. Passport
4. Your doctor's names and telephone numbers
5. Xerox copies of your regular prescriptions
6. A list of all of your credit cards and numbers
7. A list of your luggage contents (for any loss claims)

Melanie, of Long Beach, California, verifies that romantic memories are the best souvenirs of any honeymoon.

We made a mistake. We went to the Bahamas for our honeymoon, but we spent so much time buying souvenir bargains for our family members that we missed some of the relaxing and fun activities we also wanted to do. *Your* honeymoon is *your* special time for relaxed intimacy—forget the souvenirs—spend your time enjoying each other.

Do make sure to take along your camera, however, and extra rolls of film. Film at the resorts is generally priced at a premium.

Most honeymoons are planned months in advance, but what if you weren't going to honeymoon, then at the last minute decided to plan one, as Arlene, of Kansas City, Kansas, did?

One of the greatest ideas we ever heard of for a spur-of-the-moment honeymoon is the last-minute travel club. These clubs

---

BRIDAL BARGAIN

A weekend getaway honeymoon is another way to save money. Many resorts and hotels offer fabulous romantic weekend packages.

are plugged into tour operators who will discount unsold airline seats and hotel rooms rather than let them go empty. For a small membership fee, they'll pass these buys on to you. You can join immediately and call their hotline number for info on what's available from a three day stay up to six weeks. Several of these clubs include: Stand Buys (fee $45) 1-800-255-0200; Short Notice (fee $36) 1-800-638-8976; or Moment's Notice (fee $45) 212-486-0503. A company called "The Cruise Line" offers last-minute cruises with no fees at 1-800-327-3021.

Another simple last-minute strategy is to call local resorts in your area or bed and breakfast inns for a few days of quiet bliss.

Most bridal couples do not leave for their honeymoon destination until the day after the wedding. Anita, of Oakland, California, gives her testimony to this practice.

I wish we had waited until the next day to leave for our honeymoon in Europe. We left right from the reception and had only four minutes to change before our limo left for the airport. We tried to do too much all in one day and just lost complete track of the time.

Diane, of Bowling Green, Ohio, warns brides about wandering too far from home.

I strongly suggest that, for your wedding night, you choose a place that is close to your reception site. My husband and I thought we would enjoy spending our first night as husband and wife in a romantic country cabin with a fireplace. We made reservations at a quaint little resort outside of the city. Not only did we have a hard time finding it at night, we were also more tired and feeling the effects of our celebration than we realized. As a result, by the time we arrived, we were too beat to light a fire, and had to get up early in the morning to allow time to get ready and go to the airport.

Many brides and grooms should also know that when you check in at your honeymoon hotel or resort, you should say that you are newlyweds. Many facilities will have complimentary flowers, fruit, or even champagne sent to your room.

Carol, of Pueblo, Colorado, cautions brides to beware of wedding night pranksters.

We have a close circle of friends whom we refer to as the Brew Crew. They get a big kick out of playing practical jokes. Sometimes the joke is funny—but when it ruins my honeymoon it is no longer a laughing matter. When we arrived at the airport ticket desk to pick up our tickets, the agent told us that they had been canceled just the day before (our wedding day). Luckily there were extra seats still available so we were able to get on the flight. At this time, we were still unaware that this "prank" was part of a master plan. When we arrived at the hotel, and registered, the desk clerk was surprised to see two people announcing that they were newlyweds when his computer had a "single" room requested. Again, we were fully accommodated by the hotel who kept apologizing for the misunderstanding. After we finally settled in our room, there was a knock at the door and the bellboy handed my husband a telegram. It read "Glad you made the flight, hope you have a very cozy week in your single bed—Lots of Love, The Brew Crew."

Other brides would agree that after all the anxiety of the wedding day, this kind of humor is definitely inappropriate.

Brittany, of Muncie, Indiana, stresses the importance of foolproofing your wedding night.

We had reserved a room at a local all-suites hotel for our wedding night. When we arrived in our wedding attire, the clerk checked us in and gave us the key to our suite. When we opened the door, another couple was already in bed in the room. We quickly excused ourselves and returned to the desk clerk who gave us another suite down the hall from the first one. This one was still not cleaned from the last guests. The bed was unmade, the bathroom filled with dirty towels, and pizza was left over from their party. My husband was furious. This was our wedding night. We marched back to the clerk who, from the look in his eye, wished he could have crawled under the desk. He said he had no other suites available. Then we got mad. We told him we knew that hotels always kept at least one spare room available. We really caused a boisterous argument. He sheepishly found something down at the end of the last hallway, and that is where we spent what was left of our wedding night. I'm really sorry now, that after that horrible wedding night experience we didn't go away to some resort for at least the rest of that weekend.

Jean, of Dallas, warns about a "timely" arrival.

It was our wedding day. We wanted everything to be perfect. A travel agent arranged for the bridal suite at the most luxurious hotel in Dallas. I even called two weeks before the wedding to reconfirm the reservation. At 10:30 P.M., the limo picked us up at our reception site. We invited a few close friends to come with us and stopped at a few places before going to the hotel. At 12:30 A.M. we arrived at the hotel and we were told that all of the suites were booked, but they could give us a room with a fold-out couch! It appears that because they were not notified that we were arriving very late, and we failed to arrive by 12:00 A.M., they gave the suite to someone else. We called our lawyer, but he said we had no recourse.

To begin with, reserving your room with a major credit card would have insured that no one was given that room but you. If you did not show up at all at the hotel, the room cost, under a "no-show" clause, would automatically have been charged to your card. Better yet, on the morning of your wedding have your best man or another close friend go to the hotel and check in for you and give you the key to your suite—then you can rest assured that your wedding day does not end with a bleak night. I hope this sad tale will benefit future newlyweds.

Your honeymoon should be a special time for just the two of you to share in whatever way you wish to. Don't overschedule yourselves. Relax and have fun because these are the first days of the rest of your lives together. Make them special!

Epilogue

A wedding ranks among life's most traumatic events. There are really only two things that can cause a wedding day disaster. One is an act of God, and the other is a human error. There is no person alive who intentionally wants to spoil your wedding day.

It is also wise to remember that even the best-planned shortcuts can backfire. In truth, there are no real bridal bargains. You get exactly what you pay for. But there are some excellent bridal buys available if you know what to look for, and how to shop for them.

There is a secret formula: Gently mix the personalities and feelings of all who love you. Add a dash of common sense and an ounce of precaution, and you will create the wonderful wedding you have always dreamed of.